An Archangel's Gift

*A personal journey through
instinct, intuition,
research, and revelation.*

Edward Spellman

An Archangel's Gift

Copyright © Edward Spellman 2020.
All rights reserved. This book or any portion thereof may not be reproduced or used in any manner whatsoever without the express written permission of the publisher and author except for the use of brief quotations in a book review.
Copyright registered with Copyright House 2020.
First published as Uriel's Gift in 2017
Drawings and photos by Edward Spellman.

Edited by Lauren Daniels.

A CIP catalogue record for this title is available from the Australian National Library.

ISBN-13: 978-0-6485527-7-2

Edward Spellman

Acknowledgments

I would like to thank everybody who has given me positive feedback and constructive criticism over the years, especially my friends, Selina and Jarryd, for their encouragement and support.

Thank you also to all of my spiritual guides and guardians without whom I would not have written this book…without them, I would not have been here to write this book so thank you again with all my heart.

And to my editor, Lauren Daniels, I love what you have done. Thank you is simply inadequate.

Dedication

I dedicate this book to my three children, Richard, Amanda and Jason. I am continuously both proud and astounded they chose me to be their father. It is and always will be a privilege.

Also to those three facets of Spirit I met on the seventeenth of July 1996, the catalysts for my story.

Edward Spellman

Contents

Canberra 1996 to 1999

Chapter 1...My Lifeline 1
Chapter 2...Red Leaves in the Distance 17
Chapter 3...The Black Horseman 27
Chapter 4...Looking for the Black Horseman 35
Chapter 5...Personal Development Classes 47
Chapter 6...I Will Fight No More Forever 57
Chapter 7...Follow the Earthen Cascade 63
Chapter 8...Running Wolf 71
Chapter 9...The Horseman Again 75
Chapter 10...The Negative Aspects of Self 83
Chapter 11...Teacher 87
Chapter 12...Success 95
Chapter 13...The Devil's Waiting Room 99
Chapter 14...Wind Blows, Rivers Flow 107
Chapter 15...Edward 113
Chapter 16...An Invitation 119

Melbourne 1999 to 2005

Chapter 17...Bleeding Fingers 125
Chapter 18...Self-Sufficiency 137
Chapter 19...My Suit of Golden Armour 145
Chapter 20...The Emerald Cave 153
Chapter 21...Horses 161
Chapter 22...Snowballs... 167
Chapter 23...That Day 175
Chapter 24...Barren Ground 185
Chapter 25...Not Dead Again?.. 191
Chapter 26...A Grey Streetscape 203
Chapter 27...Sitting in a Forest Clearing......................... 209

Edward Spellman

South East Queensland 2005 to 2016

Chapter 28...Just a Distraction..219
Chapter 29...Not That Way 223
Chapter 30...Spiritual Amnesia and Confusion..............227
Chapter 31...Your Past Points to Your Path 231
Chapter 32...The Holy Spirit as a Dove............................237
Chapter 33...Help 243
Chapter 34...A Leap of Faith..255
Chapter 35...What If This Is Just All Boot Camp? 259
Chapter 36...Muddy Water 265
Chapter 37...Impatience 273
Chapter 38...The Framework for the Rest of My Life 279
Chapter 39...The Stone Passageway 283
Chapter 40...The Farmer and His Sheep 289
Chapter 41...God's Workshop 293
Chapter 42...Buried in a Landslide 297
Chapter 43...The Farmer, His Son and the Knight 301
Chapter 44...Redcliffe Lagoon 305
Chapter 45...Follow the Ripples 311
Chapter 46...Why Not Me? 315
Epilogue………………………………...……………..….323
About the Author……………………………………..….325

Contents

Drawings:

My Lifeline by Edward Spellman, 2016 9
Follow the Earthen Cascade by Edward Spellman, 2016 66

Photographs:

The Prophecy Shield by Edward Spellman, 2016 233
My Workshop 327

Edward Spellman

Canberra

1996 to 1999

An Archangel's Gift

Chapter 1
My Lifeline

I died on the seventeenth of July 1996—life became very interesting after that.

It was a Wednesday night and although I didn't know it at the time, I had just ten seconds left until I died.

I was driving east on William Hovel Drive heading toward the intersection with Coulter Drive in Canberra, Australia's capital city. It was a dark night with sunset about an hour earlier and not much moonlight. The traffic was light and the roads were dry.

Up ahead, the intersection was well lit. There was only one car behind me, which was slowly getting closer. I kept an eye out for kangaroos on the road—and I thought about the tai chi class I was driving to that night and that I liked the instructors.

Nine seconds.

An Archangel's Gift

I was smiling, thinking about where I was in my life compared to where I had been. It was just two and a half years since my marriage broke up. Back then, I was thrown into a dark depression after I found a note left on my pillow one Monday morning in January 1994. Those seven words burned their way into my mind, heart and soul: *Don't be here when I get home.*

The next morning, I found another note. "I'm serious, I don't love you. Don't be here when I get home."

My eldest son was home when I left with a few things to go stay with my mother. That broke me.

But a lot had changed since then.

Eight seconds.

I hadn't handled it well. It felt like my three children were taken from me. I didn't know who I was anymore. I was still their father, but I wondered if I would ever see them again.

I remembered how I wept while I drove during the separation, sobbing and pressing the accelerator as I approached a notorious right-angled bend on top of the Clyde Mountain.

I remembered the strong, calm, male voice that spoke to me then. *"Do you want your children to feel like this?"*

There was no one else there, at least no one physical.

Edward Spellman

Seven seconds.

In response to the voice, I had lifted my foot off the accelerator of the old Mitsubishi ute and slowed to make the bend safely.

That voice! I'd heard it before. It had called my name when I was an apprentice bricklayer. I was working in a lift-well when, on hearing my name called, I stepped in the direction of the voice but no one was there; only me on the entire second floor where I was working.

Six seconds.

It was the same voice, I had thought. That voice had made me step away from where I was working right before a lump of concrete a little bigger than my head hit the spot I'd just vacated, putting a large dint on the plywood deck. That lump of concrete would have killed me instantly.

On my way to tai chi as I approached the intersection, I wondered why I was remembering that voice. I hadn't thought about those incidents in a long time, and I had never thought they were related.

I also didn't know that the one who had spoken to me was waiting for me just down the road.

An Archangel's Gift

Five seconds.

Before going to my tai chi class, I wanted to stop by my workshop and pick up materials for work the following day. Work was wonderful, better than I could ever have hoped. I had jobs booked for the rest of that year and my business was finally booming again after all the lean years.

As I came to the intersection, I was thinking about the difference between the car I was driving, a new Holden Rodeo 4x4, and the old ute I had almost driven off the Clyde two and a half years ago. I liked the Holden. I was forty-one years old and it was the first new car I'd ever had.

Four seconds.

I looked in the side mirror past the tradesman's trailer I was towing and only one set of headlights still hung behind me. I looked ahead. A white station wagon approached the intersection from the left, on the Coulter Drive side. It was going quite slowly with plenty of time to stop at the give way sign. That was good because I didn't have time to stop for them.

Three seconds.

The station wagon was almost at the white line, so they should have been stopping. They weren't moving very fast, just creeping into the intersection.

I still thought they were going to stop but they just kept moving forward as though they couldn't see me. If I slammed on my brakes, I would have slid straight into them and killed whoever was driving because they were right in front of me. If I swerved, and the trailer I was towing jackknifed, it would have been the end of me.

I chose.

The thought of being responsible for killing someone was something I couldn't cope with, so I swerved.

Two seconds.

The white station wagon collided with the front left hand corner of my car.

As I swerved, the impact pushed the front of my car even more to the right while the trailer, weighing at least a ton, pushed the back of my car forward until it was at a right angle to the direction I was travelling. The two left hand wheels slammed into the concrete curb as the trailer lifted off the ground and arced forward, throwing me into a sideways spin while snapping the supposedly unbreakable tow-bar and flying off into the distance, spilling materials and tools as it went.

An Archangel's Gift

One second.

As my car began its journey through the air, time slipped into slow motion. Below me, through the windscreen, I watched the grass on the traffic island spiral across my vision. My three children's faces drifted before my eyes and I couldn't help but smile as I relived their births and the moment they had opened their eyes for the first time.

I was saying goodbye.

The ground drifted closer and I instinctively raised my right arm to protect my eyes as time slipped back to normal. My head and right arm slammed through the window; my arm slapped the ground as the car rolled and…

…suddenly everything was calm…not just calm but peaceful in a way that I find words impossible to describe…it felt like a quiet pool at the end of some noisy rapids but much, much more than that…

I watched from above as my car rolled one final time amongst the dust and debris, rocked from side to side, then settled on its wheels. I looked down on my physical body still strapped into the driver's seat.

Jesus was watching with me, as was an Archangel—a being of light I came to know as Uriel, and there was another that I chose to call Farronell. The three of them were pure light and, for a moment, they showed me what I looked like to them, and I saw myself as pure light as well. There was no difference between us.

Below, a young woman, the driver of the white station wagon, shaking and terrified but unharmed, was helped from her vehicle by two more women and a man who had stopped at the scene. She stood there shaking, holding herself and was supported by the two women. She looked stunned and frightened, unable as yet to comprehend what happened. She stared at the wreck of my car in a daze.

The two women comforted her as the man walked to my car, reached in through the broken window and turned off the engine. I watched as he checked me for signs of life. Finding none, he walked back to where the three women stood and said. "The other driver's dead."

It didn't feel strange at all to see someone pronounce me dead.

While I watched this scene play out before me, Jesus, Uriel and Farronell showed me why I was there, where I was up to in this life and how it connected to both past and future lives. They also showed me this life and all it held for me, past, present and future.

Then I was given the choice to either stay with them or return to my life as Edward Spellman. I was given the information I required to make an informed decision, with the understanding that should I choose to return to my life, I would temporarily forfeit some of what they had shown me as, if I were to go back with all of the knowledge it would detrimentally effect how I interacted with the world. Those memories would be given back to me in time, when my mind could handle it.

Also, if I chose to return, I would not be empty-handed. I would return with a gift and the promise of something to draw me forward in life. Something that I would understand instantly and yet my understanding of it would deepen over time.

I chose to return.

And I woke with a vision of my lifeline accompanied by a promise, and to immense pain.

The vision and the sense of those three beings lingered as I found myself back in the car. It was so simple, and yet it held so much hope for the future. I knew instantly that although I was slumped there busted and broken and my business was dead in the dust with the extent of these injuries, everything would be fine.

The vision showed my life before and up to the accident as a line that ran parallel to an edge, the accident as a squiggly line, and my life after the accident as a line that ran off in a completely different direction.

Accompanying the vision of my lifeline there were those three beings—beings of Light?

Edward Spellman

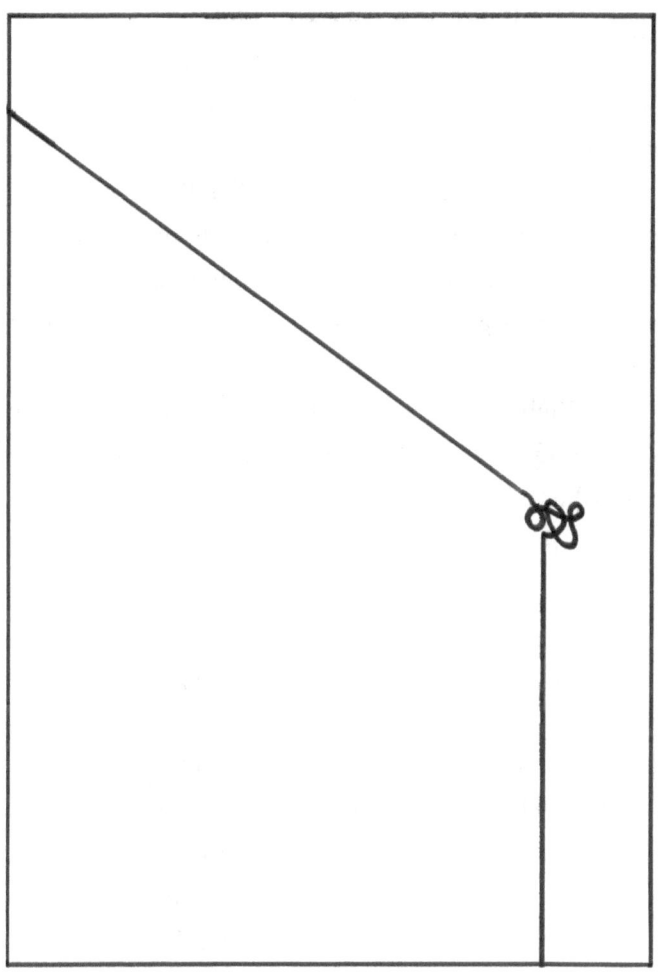

My Lifeline by Edward Spellman, 2016.

Still in the car, I tried to understand what they were…consciousness of Light? They all felt familiar, like I should have known their names, names that were on the tip of my tongue.

Whoever they were, I knew that the lifeline vision and the accompanying promise and hope came from them, and yet, they also made me feel uncomfortable because of who they were and what it all meant for my perceptions of reality.

Right then in the car, I noticed that my right arm dangled by my side and while the pain was severe everywhere else, I couldn't feel it at all.

Turn off the engine. I thought through the pain.
That's weird; it is off.

Strange visions of a man walking up to my car, leaning in through the broken window, and turning off my ignition returned to my mind. I wondered how I could have remembered seeing someone lean in and turn off the ignition, and better yet, I remembered it as though I had seen it from above when I was still sitting in the car.

Everything hurt, even breathing. My mind flitted between the vision, praying for the ambulance to get there, and back again.

Another memory drifted through my mind. Words, teasing me from a distance, coming closer, what were they?
The other driver's dead.

Oh shit! I've killed someone. Tears rolled down my cheeks and mixed with my blood.

Take inventory. I told myself. *You've done first aid for years and you know not to move because you've just had a head injury but you can tense your muscles without moving to see how much damage there is.*

Ok, toes first.

If I could wriggle my toes, it meant my back wasn't broken. So I tentatively moved my toes and there was no specifically associated pain. That was good.

Then I softly, slowly, scrunched my feet up. No pain from that...

Then I rolled my ankles as much as I could without moving the rest of my legs, settled the balls of my feet on the floor and slowly tensed my calf muscles, then thighs and buttocks without causing myself any pain.

It was a relief to have found nothing damaged below my waist so I kept going. I rolled my stomach muscles and expanded my chest. My stomach felt fine but my chest hurt when I tried to take a deep breath...but shallow breathing was fine.

I moved my left hand and fingers. No problem. I tried the left arm and that was good too.

My right arm began to feel warm and wet through the pain as it dangled down beside the seat. I couldn't move it at all. I took my right wrist gently in my left hand and moved it slowly into my lap for support. That hurt. It felt mangled. The right hand side of my head ached and my right ear also felt like it had been torn off. The right hand side of my body was soaked in blood from gashes along my arm, neck and head.

I longed for the ambulance.

Tears fell as I thought again of the other driver being killed.

Sirens bawled in the night and faded. Brakes screamed.

I prayed through the pain that it was the ambulance as I continued to take slow steady breaths and hold my right elbow with my left hand.

I still hadn't opened my eyes.

Car doors slammed and I heard people running.

Someone yelled. "Get him out of there!"

Thank God. I thought. *They're here. As soon as they get the other driver out, they will look after me.*

Then a crowbar slammed into my car door.

An insistent, urgent voice yelled again. "Get him out!"

I opened my eyes and said. "Get the other driver out first. I'm okay."

Then came a sudden moment of silence followed by the same voice, shocked this time. "He's alive! Get him out!"

The crowbar slammed into the door again and again until the door ripped open.

I asked. "How's the other driver?

The ambulance officer said. "Don't worry about the other driver. Are you ok? Can you move?"

"Yes, I can move."

"Do you think you can get out with our help?"

"Yes."

"First we'll get this neck brace on."

"How's the other driver?" I asked again.

Ignoring my question, he said. "Just move slowly and step out of the car. We'll help you. Do you think you can walk to the ambulance with our help?"

"Yes, I can do that. How's the other driver?" I asked again as we walked toward the ambulance.

"The other driver's fine. Just keep walking."

I needed to know how the other driver was—I was still worried that I'd killed someone.

"We have to get you into the ambulance; just keep walking."

"No!"

I stopped and planted my feet stubbornly as best I could, still hearing those words echoing through my mind. "The other driver's dead." I needed to see for myself. "I'm not going anywhere until you take me to the other driver."

I could hear the frustration in their voices as they realised I was not moving until I saw the other driver.

"You're not going anywhere! Just stay here and we'll bring her to you."

She was young, early twenties maybe. Her eyes were wide and scared and there were tears on her face. She had one arm in a sling and was supported by two women.

As soon as I saw her expression, I knew she thought she had killed me, just as I thought I had killed her.

"It's okay!" I said. "I'm all right. It was just an accident. Nobody's fault." I looked toward her arm held in a sling and asked. "Are you okay?"

Unable to speak from the shock, she nodded.

The ambulance officer saw my concern and said, "The sling is just a precaution."

I was happy then. I let them walk me to the ambulance and sat in the back.

Sitting there, looking in the direction of the wreck of my car, I started to laugh, which caused more pain.

"Get him a blanket." The ambulance officer said to his partner.

"It's okay. I don't need a blanket."

"Yes, you do. You're going into shock."

"What makes you think I'm going into shock?"

"You're laughing. That doesn't make any sense."

I smiled and pointed, with my left hand, past the wreck of my life…my car, my trailer full of work materials. "I just walked out of that."

That pacified him but I wasn't looking at the wreck. I was gazing in that direction and still seeing the vision of my lifeline. I was thinking about the three beings and the promise that came with them.

What also made me laugh was that even though my business lay wrecked before me, and I couldn't see any way to save it because it depended on me doing the physical work, it somehow didn't matter. I was alive.

While sitting in the back of the ambulance, the officers introduced me to the pain whistle. I didn't know what was in that thing, but I was glad they had it. As I breathed through the whistle, the pain drifted away and I began to wonder what my future held. I thought I would wake up the next day and everything would be different.

They rushed me to the hospital for x-rays, bandages, stitches and shined lights in my eyes. I usually don't like doctors much but that night, I was happy to let them do their thing.

Surprisingly I had no broken bones, just a lot of soft tissue damage and the feeling started to return to my right arm.

I got home that night at around 11:00. The doctors only let me go home on the condition my girlfriend at the time, a nurse, stayed with me for the night.

I drifted off to sleep looking at the vision of my lifeline and considering the promise. This promise wasn't like, *I promise not to eat the last piece of cake,* or, *I promise to clean my room.*

An Archangel's Gift

It was more a promise like the first blush of crimson on the horizon is the promise of a new dawn, and that new dawn promises a new day full of wonder and love and fun. It promised something magickal, and it promised something new and different in a way that felt like a smile.

As I lay there, the promise gripped and held me, just as it would for the rest of my life. The promise drew me forward.

Chapter 2
Red Leaves in the Distance

I awoke the next morning to see an aerial view of the accident and my lifeline replay in my mind with the three 'beings of Light' in attendance; the promise shining.

I didn't see the collision itself: it started with my car already rolling. It came to a stop and soon after a man walked over to the wreck, reached in through the broken window and turned off the ignition. He checked me for signs of life then walked back to where three women stood, two supporting another between them, and said. "The other driver's dead."

I wondered why I kept seeing it. I was the other driver and as far as I could tell, I wasn't dead.

Three beings of Light flashed through my mind.
What do they want?

I tried to push the memory of them and the sense I had of their identities into the back of my mind. I found their appearance confronting so instead I held tight to the vision of my lifeline and the promise; both of which gave me a feeling of calm and that all was good with my life.

I knew I needed to come up with a plan. First I unloaded all of my work because not only was I injured and had lost my car and trailer, I wanted to be ready to take the new direction I was promised by the beings of Light.

A few days passed and I continued to pass on work, although several of my client builders were unhappy with me.

On the fourth day after the accident, the pain hit in earnest and I had to start using the painkillers I was given at the hospital.

I couldn't get out of bed on the fifth morning until half an hour after taking the painkillers, and then it took all of my energy just to go to the bathroom and have a drink of water. I spent most of the day just trying not to move.

In the days following the accident, my girlfriend started acting a little strange, even though I never told her about my experience. She kept ringing me and asking. "Do you want to break up with me?"

I assured her that I didn't want to break up with her and she settled down and we had a good chat.

Then the next night, however, she asked again. It was confusing as my head was still spinning from the accident, the lifeline vision, pain, three beings of Light, the promise and more pain if I did things like breathe or move.

On top of that, some of the builders had started to hound me to work for them. I told them I couldn't because I was injured. I didn't tell them I didn't want to do it because I had seen a vision of my lifeline which had shown my life taking a completely different direction.

To distract myself from the builders and my girlfriend, I contacted a friend in Perth who I had met the year before on a camel trek in the Simpson Desert and sent some photos of my smashed up ute.

My girlfriend called again. "Do you want to break up with me?"

"No, of course not." I replied.

I wasn't sure what was going on. My girlfriend was harassing me and the vision of my lifeline teased me every moment, even while I was asleep. I still wasn't game to tell anybody what had happened to me, as I was having trouble accepting it myself.

As my girlfriend enquired anxiously about our relationship and I was trying to reassure her, I was also trying to deal with the relentless visions.

A builder knocked on my door. When I answered, he demanded I do a job I had agreed to do for him before the accident. He didn't understand that I was incapable at the time. My body hurt; everything hurt.

My girlfriend called again wanting reassurance.

Visions of my lifeline chased me. The promise haunted and teased me.

Another builder came to the house.

My girlfriend called again even though I'd repeatedly assured her I didn't want our relationship to end.

I was pretty sure I was going nuts when I got an invitation from the friend in Perth I'd sent the photos to. She invited me to go over for ten days' R&R so I booked my flights.

My girlfriend called. "Do you want to break up with me?"

By then, I was fed up. "Oh for God's sake, yes!" I said and hung up the phone.

She called back. "We need to talk. We have issues."

"You have issues. Goodbye." I hung up and unplugged the phone.

And I was off to Perth.

Was I running away?

You bet I was.

I needed to feel safe and distance was what I craved. Perth was about as far away as I could get and still be in the same country.

I needed time to think. I needed time to try and work out what was happening.

I spent ten days sightseeing in Western Australia with a friend and got a chance to breathe; to reflect and take in everything that had happened.

The lifeline vision still consumed me, although I didn't mention it to my friend, but I did my best to grapple with it.

It told me that my life would change direction and that that direction would be the most positive, prosperous and joy filled experience, but I had no idea how to get there.

Two months passed and still this elusive new direction stayed out of reach. I hadn't put any effort into getting back to work because I was waiting for my new direction—but it didn't come. I decided that I had better do something while I waited.

I bought a second-hand Nissan Patrol 4X4 and had another trailer set up to my specifications so I could at least appear to be doing something constructive and attempting to make a living, even though my heart wasn't in it.

I still hadn't told anyone about the vision. I already thought I was crazy, so why would anyone else have thought any different? And yet, even though I thought I was crazy, I still believed both the vision and the promise.

For my first attempt to get back to work, I did a small job. What would previously have taken an hour or two at most, took me a full day and a week to get over the physical pain of it.

Even though I tried to ignore the vision and its promise so I could get back into work, I found my mind continually occupied with possibilities of the new direction I was shown.

I tried to do some tai chi but I quickly discovered that my balance was shot and all my muscles were out of sync. I couldn't even lift my arms above my shoulders.

My solicitor asked me to keep a diary for my insurance claim. She said that if I could show that I was getting worse rather than better, I would get considerably more money. The idea was to write in my diary every day that I was feeling worse, and in more pain, than I had the day before.

I tried that for about ten days and my solicitor was right. I did feel worse every day, so I stopped and thought about it for a while and then threw that diary in the bin where it belonged and bought a new one.

The very next morning I made my first entry in my new diary. "Today I feel a little better than I did yesterday."

I kept that up for ten days and every day, I felt a little better.

That was enough for me to believe I could make myself better or worse, so that diary went the same way as the other, and then I just decided to feel a little better each day. It worked, although much more slowly than I wanted.

Each time I did a job, I could work a little better. My body hurt a little less and my recuperation was a little shorter, but I was still a long way from making a living. I was only doing odd jobs and they had to be small, simple and within my physical limitations. I often knocked back some really good jobs because I simply wasn't capable at the time.

Christmas came and went, and then it was 3a.m. on New Year's Day.

I had worked the day before and gone out for New Year's Eve with a friend. I didn't drink because I was driving and exhausted.

After the celebrations, I dropped my friend off at her place and went home. When I got there, I went into my house but didn't turn on any lights. I just went straight to bed and sat on the edge; I took a deep slow breath and enjoyed the silence before sleep.

As I sat there in the dark with my eyes closed, breathing slowly, questions drifted across my mind. The vision of my lifeline appeared again along with its promise.

Who am I?

Why am I here?

What's happening to me?

I took another breath, and as I exhaled, I saw with my eyes closed, way off in the distance and only just discernible, a group of small red dots scattered across a square. It reminded me of a window on a distant wall seen at night. I couldn't see any pattern, only that the dots were scattered across a rough square about half the size of a postage stamp.

Curious, I attempted a closer look. I took a deep breath, relaxed a little more, and allowed my consciousness to fall toward them; but the dots retreated almost out of sight. I tried three times with the same result.

I stopped trying to get closer and just relaxed, wondering how to get a closer look at the red dots, especially since it felt like they wanted me to. Then, on an impulse—or did I hear a voice suggest it? —I tried the opposite.

Again I took a deep breath and allowed my consciousness to fall, but this time backwards into myself and away from the red dots. The effect was immediate, and a little strange as it felt like my conscious awareness split in two. One part fell into myself—which was like falling into a void that contained nothing and yet everything at the same time. The other part stayed where it was and the red dots rushed forward to fill my field of vision.

I saw a body of clear still water and sprinkled all across its surface were the red dots, which I now saw were red leaves. It was strange but I recognised the leaves. They were the leaves of a Chinese elm tree, one of my favourite trees, but I had never seen its leaves that colour before.

At the centre of the pool and just a little below the surface, there was a beautiful, androgynous, golden face. I knew it had something to do with, or was in some way, Jesus, while at the same time, it was much more than that.

As I watched, molecules of water vapour coalesced high above the surface. Soon, the single drop that formed became too heavy to stay where it was and broke free to take its inevitable journey. The drop hit the water directly above the golden face sending ripples out across the entire surface of the pool. As I watched that single drop take shape and fall, it felt familiar but in a way that I didn't understand at first. It felt very personal.

Then suddenly I understood: I was the drop.

As I drifted off to sleep I forgot the three questions I'd had before I saw the vision.

Instead, I wondered what this vision meant and what it had to do with the glimpse of my lifeline.

An Archangel's Gift

Chapter 3
The Black Horseman

In the morning, I thought about the vision I saw just before bed. I understood some of it and knew I was the drop. I was also starting to wonder if all this had something to do with me being hit in the head and if something was wrong with me.

I didn't know what the water was—all I knew was that it was endless in both breadth and depth. I wondered again why I was seeing weird stuff like this.

I recognised the leaves, although they were a colour I had never seen on those particular trees, they don't do autumn colours.

Jesus? What the...? I wasn't even sure if I believed in Jesus, so how could I have a vision that reminds me of him?

I watched the drop form and fall then break free from whatever was holding it back and set off on a journey that was both natural and inevitable. Also, the drop falling into the body of water meant a return to its source.

When the drop hit the water, it sent ripples across the entire surface.

I did some research on the Chinese elm and saw that it had spread to all the continents on Earth except Antarctica. I had no idea how that could be relevant.

I didn't know what the golden face represented, except that it had something to do with Jesus and it was very important. I felt that the blood red leaves symbolised something to do with my DNA.

None of this seemed to tell me anything about the new direction I was looking for however, and if it did, I didn't understand it.

I felt like I'd missed something.

I wondered about the meaning of the emptiness inside myself, and also about the vision moving away as I tried to get closer. When I tried to get closer, it retreated. That felt sort of external, like it was happening outside of myself. Then, when I reversed what I was doing, and tried falling into myself, everything became clear and close.

I realised I had to look inside myself to find whatever it was that I was looking for.

I suppose it would have helped a little if I had known what I was looking for.

After spending the next three weeks trying to figure out my visions, I decided to take a friend up on an offer to go stay with her. I'd been there maybe two days, when her sister, Kelly, asked me to give her a lift to her babysitting job.

We were on our way when all of a sudden, as well as being aware of driving, the sound of the Nissan's engine, the air conditioner, the other cars, the shops we passed and all the things I saw on a busy street, my reality was overlaid and integrated with another; another body, another time. Neither reality was more dominant than the other. I was simultaneously both here and there, now and then.

Spring sunshine filled the countryside around me as a gentle breeze moved the grass and kissed the new growth on the ancient oaks. I sat astride a black stallion that flexed his muscles beneath me, I felt his chest expand as he inhaled, snorted and pulled at the reins. His hooves churned the fertile soil of the forest edge; he was eager to be off but we held back; an air of expectancy pervaded the grove where a group waited. A dozen young warriors surrounded me, mounted, ready. I was part of a group of horsemen who were dressed in homespun cloth and leather. None of us carried weapons, nor wore any amour, and yet there was not one amongst us that would normally go about unarmed, as we were warriors. Each of us intent on the tree line at the far side of the meadow.

Through the trees to my left, I glimpsed a spring fair. Laughter and the smells of animals and fresh cooked food drifted on the air.

I drew a breath and noticed my young, muscular body, wondering how it could be me whilst feeling calm about what I felt.

About twenty paces away, a group of men and women were dressed in medieval garb as we were, watching a game unfold. I felt my heart racing. The blood coursed through my veins and I felt a muscle tone in my body that I hadn't felt for years, if ever, in this life.

Those who watched talked amongst themselves, sharing their attention between the young men on horseback and the trees on the far side of a field scattered with mauve, yellow and white wildflowers, glistening with dew in the early morning sunlight.

Nearby, a nine-year-old boy lead a sow, a light rope tied around one of her back legs, half a dozen piglets followed, never far from their mother. He knew he was not supposed to be here and yet could not resist a closer look at his heroes.

I could smell the horses, the men and the fresh turned earth mixed with the scent of flowers. I could taste the earth on my tongue. A branch creaked in the wind. Leaves rustled. One of the women watching laughed light heartedly.

A group of maidens emerged from the trees that bordered the far side of the meadow and we watched them. Their group was equal in number to ours. One maiden, to the far right of the group held my attention. I watched her talking to her companions, laughing, slowly walking closer.

Tall and proud, she stood. Her golden hair in braids that reached to her slim waist, her long skirts were hitched up between her legs and through a belt at the waist as were the skirts of her companions, for ease of running; she had a natural born athleticism and suppleness that made my heart sing.

As the women came into view, they seemed unaware of us; they laughed and talked as they walked out into the open meadow.

All of a sudden they noticed us for the first time and one of them let out an ululating cry that was taken up by the entire group. Then, with a shout of defiance and challenge in their voices, they all turned and fled. As would a herd of deer that had spied the hunt, they scattered.

Swift those handsome maidens were, and swiftest of all, the one that held my eye. The instant the warning was sounded by the young women, spurs dug into horses' ribs and clods of soft black earth flew from hooves as we surged forward. Battle cries filled the air. Instantly my black horse leapt ahead. He knew this game well. Guided only by my knees, we gave chase.

Each of those young warriors was intent on a different maiden. The young women sped across the open meadow without looking back toward the cover of the trees.

As I galloped toward my chosen, I leant to my left side, hooking my arm and as I came up behind and to the right of her, I gave voice to the signal. She leapt and pivoted to her right, hooking her left arm in mine, and swung up behind my saddle with practiced ease.

That's when Kelly said. "Let me off just past this next telephone pole. It's that red brick house on the left."

I pulled the Nissan over to the side of the road.

"OK, do you need a lift home after work?"

"No, thanks. I'll make my own way. See ya. Bye."

As Kelly got out of the car I realised she hadn't seen any of what I had, even though to me it had been as real and solid as sitting there in the car.

OK. So, what just happened to me? How is it possible to be in two places, and in two times, at the same time?

Then I wondered how I could be so calm when it was pretty obvious that I had lost my mind.

I thought it was supposed to be impossible to be in two places, let alone two times at the same time. Apparently not, because it just happened.

Whoever I was in that time, I was a lot fitter. I could feel the blood in my veins. I felt the air move through my lungs. I felt the horse between my legs while in this life, horses and I were not that familiar. Then, I was born to the saddle. It didn't feel at all like I was in another person's body, it felt like it was me.

But I couldn't make sense of it, even my calm reaction puzzled me as it was again, outside of anything I recalled experiencing. Then again, I saw that vision with the red leaves, the vision of my lifeline, and the three beings of light from above the car accident that I didn't talk about.

In the back of my mind, I stored all of the experiences that were uncomfortable: the ones that made me doubt my sanity.

An Archangel's Gift

Chapter 4

Looking for the Black Horseman

During the drive back to Canberra from Cooma the following day, I kept repeating a question in my mind. *Who is the black horseman?*

I called him the black horseman because his hair, his clothes and his horse were black. *How did, whatever that was, happen? Why did it happen?* And I wanted to know who he was.

On reaching Canberra, I crossed Lake Burley Griffin on Kings Avenue Bridge, then turned left onto Parke's Way, which would have given me a straight run almost all the way home. Then I heard that soft voice in the depths of my mind.

"Take the next right."

So I took the next right onto Coranderrk Street. I wasn't sure why I followed the directions, but I did.

What now? I asked and immediately saw an image of a woman with long, straight, blond hair standing behind a glass display case with a cash register on it.

I remembered her; I'd seen her last year as I was walking past the carousel in the center of the intersection of Bunda and Petrie Streets in Civic. I remembered looking through the door of a shop as I walked past and saw the woman I was being shown, although I had never been in that particular shop and I had never met her.

I felt amused at getting directions in my mind so I followed them and headed for the Griffin Centre car park. It was only a short walk through Garema Place and down Bunda Street to the shop I had just seen.

As I got to where the shop was, it was gone.

Then I wondered if I shouldn't listen to the soft voices in the back of my mind. They didn't seem to know what they were talking about.

An image of a coffee shop I liked popped into my mind so I decided that I'd have a coffee instead of looking for someone who may or may not exist.

I turned around and drifted back to Garema Place, window-shopping along the way.

I walked slowly and saw an alcove with a staircase leading up to the first floor. A glass fronted display case hung on the wall containing crystals, jewelry and tarot cards.

Without any particular intent, I walked up the stairs wondering what was up there. Through the first door, I found crystals, jewelry, tarot cards, clothing and lots more and was still amused at following these directions. I looked at some crystals and wondered at the properties attributed to them.

Someone stood at the counter and I was aware of the person out of my peripheral vision but I hadn't looked that way. I didn't make eye contact with sales people unless I wanted to buy something.

I was about to leave for my coffee when a quiet female voice asked. "Is there anything I can help you with?"

I turned toward the voice with my polite. *No, thank you.* On the tip of my tongue but it didn't get any further because I was looking at exactly who I had seen in the car.

What now? I wondered.

The woman with the blonde hair stood before me and I couldn't help but ask her. "Did you have a shop down by the carousel?"

"Yes, I moved here last year."

Then she said the strangest thing. "How's your book going?"

I was stunned. "Um, I'm not writing a book. I don't know anything about writing." The whole idea of writing a book made me more than uncomfortable. It scared me.

She looked at me with a little half smile like she knew something I didn't and said. "You will. I can see it in your aura."

As I walked out of there, having forgotten all about coffee I thought. *Me! Write a book. I don't think so! Maybe she was just angling for a sale?*

Over the next few weeks, the black horseman was constantly on my mind.

On a Friday night, about three weeks after I'd found that shop, work was finished and it was time to relax. I wondered if I should go get a bottle of wine to have with the steak I was having for dinner.

I was just sitting there, watching the news as a hole in time and space opened up where the television had been.

The hairs on the back of my neck stood up as I shivered and half-finished expletives fell out of my slack-jawed mouth. "Oh fu–! Oh Go–! Oh Je–! Oh shit! Not him! Please, please, please, not him! Anybody but him! Oh shhiit! Didn't happen! Didn't happen! Didn't happen!"

Time and space had opened up in my lounge room. I was no longer seeing the news. I was looking at a young boy, maybe six, squatting in the corner, with his back to me, in his father's workshop, playing with a couple of pieces of wood.

And I knew. I knew in the depths of my soul who it was.

Edward Spellman

That was the most scared I had ever been in my life, I got an instant headache and the muscles in my back and neck tensed and locked up with the fear.

After the moment ended, I wondered why he was chasing me and what I had done wrong. I remembered when I was twelve and took down my crucifix and put it away in a cupboard because I didn't get what I wanted for my birthday. I had blamed him because I'd prayed to him for it.

I wondered if I was going crazy. I wondered if I should have told someone or should have kept it all to myself.

To distract myself, I focused on other things. I spent all of my waking hours trying to figure out what was going on while trying to forget that Friday night. I went to the local mall thinking I might see a movie. As I walked past some shops, I passed a group of psychics doing their thing.

I laughed at the idea of seeking answers from them, being the skeptic that I was. I walked slowly, thinking about whether or not they could help me, then telling myself not to be stupid.

There were six psychic readers, four women and two men. Some of them were trying to catch a customer's eyes. One of the men and one of the women were dealing their cards, looking them over, reading them I suppose, then gathering them up and doing it all again.

I walked past without stopping and thought to myself. *Argh! It's all rubbish. Don't be silly. How could they know about the horseman?*

I walked up one side of the mall heading for the movies, crossed over to the other side of the concourse, and turned back the other way and headed toward the tarot readers. I felt drawn to them.

Again I walked past, although this time a woman who was dealing cards caught my eye. Again I told myself not to be silly and sped up to get away faster.

I soon slowed down, my curiosity got the better of me, and I headed back. This time I asked the woman who had caught my eye. "How much for a reading?"

"Twenty dollars for fifteen minutes."

"OK."

So I sat for a tarot reading.

Having given her no other information than my first name and date of birth, I waited to see where it would lead.

She gave me information that she should not have been able too, so I had to reassess my opinion of psychics. The information that came left no doubt that she had a different view of the world.

The psychic, puzzled, told me that she saw me on a camel dressed in khaki and wearing a camouflaged hat. "Maybe you were a soldier in a past life?"

But she described my camel trek through the Simpson Desert of central Australia a couple of years earlier. During the trek, I had been dressed as she described.

After that, I had to ask about the black horseman.

"I'm sorry but the cards aren't showing me anything about your horseman."

A month after that boy had turned up in my lounge room, I was finally calm enough to put it behind me. I told no one about it, since I still thought they would lock me up if they knew.

La, la, la, everything's good.

Just put it under the rock in the back of my mind and forget about it. Done!

And then. *Oh shit! He's back!*

This time, as an adult, he showed me just his head and shoulders. He looked over his right shoulder at me. He had a twinkle in his brown eyes and a smile. He gave me a message. *"I know something about you that you don't know and you're really going to like it."*

Then he was gone.

Again I tried to convince myself that it didn't happen.

An Archangel's Gift

When he looked at me, I felt infinite patience, compassion and love. He looked at me like a father looking at the son he loves.

So why did that frighten me so much?

I kept going back to the same spiritual shop with the horseman in mind. I hadn't found out anything except that the woman who owned the shop was named Freyja and she reminded me that there was a book in my aura.

After one of my visits to her shop, and not long after seeing *him* for the second time, I was sitting in a coffee shop in East Row in the city. I had my back to the wall; my eyes were wide and scared. *Could they tell? Did they know I was crazy?* I wondered how long it would be before I got locked up.

The waitress came over with my coffee.

Be cool. Can she tell I'm completely crazy?

"Cappuccino, sir."

I nodded. "Thank you."

She didn't seem to notice that I was nuts.

An old song flittered through my mind. *They're coming to take you away, ha, ha, he, he, ho, ho...*

People walked past the windows of the coffee shop, traffic moved slowly, and *he* came again.

This time he showed me all of him. He was standing at a workbench, making something out of wood.

Again he looked at me over his right shoulder. I could hear him talking to me. *"I know something about you that you don't know and you are going to like it very much. It will bring you joy."*

From him, I got the same sense of infinite patience, compassion and love that I felt before.

And I had the same reaction.

Run away! Hide! Not happening! La, la, la.

Again I spent the next month convincing myself that it was all just a dream or something. Anything other than what it actually was.

After four weeks, I was relatively calm, having hidden the experiences nicely in the back of my mind. There were others back there from New Year's Day and then there was the car accident stuff. I did want to know what was going on and I wasn't game to talk to anybody about it.

I decided that, as it seemed like no one else could tell I'd gone crazy and saw visions, I would just go on with my life pretending they didn't happen.

So I was at home again, just sitting in my lounge room staring into space when *he* showed himself for the fourth time.

And again he turned his head to the right, looked me in the eyes and smiled at me with such a depth of patience, compassion and love that it touched me to the depths of my soul.

It's hard to describe the depths of emotion I felt. Tears streamed down my cheeks as I choked up with emotion from feeling his presence. I'd have fallen down if I wasn't already sitting, as all of the strength drained from my body. I began to sob. Deep, profound emotions came up from within my chest as I looked into those deep brown eyes.

As I looked into Jesus' eyes, I saw that his body was covered in blood and sweat and racked with pain as he hung nailed to the cross. I realised that I couldn't do this anymore; I couldn't pretend that he was not there with me, and that this wasn't happening to me.

My breath shuddered and, as he watched me from the cross, I sobbed.

I believe. I believe.

My heart burst and I could no longer contain my emotions as I felt him look into my soul.

He could see me.

He saw more of me than I ever could.

And with that same amused smile on his face, he gave me the same message as before. *"I know something about you that you don't know and you are going to like it very much. It will bring you joy."*

And he was gone.

Edward Spellman

I just sat, sobbing. Tears ran down my face.

I sat a long time wondering. *Why is this happening to me?*

An Archangel's Gift

Chapter 5

Personal Development Classes

Over the next few days, the acceptance of what I saw caused a sense of calm to come over me. I still thought I was probably crazy but it didn't matter anymore.

I returned to Freyja's shop and she suggested that I join some personal development classes that ran in one of her back rooms on Thursday nights. It seemed like a good idea but I wanted to think about it.

I debated doing the classes for a week then had my first class the following Thursday, run by a guy named Jayson and it was completely out of my comfort zone.

But I discovered something unexpected in that first class. Jayson was a medium, or trance channel, which means he went into trance and spiritual entities spoke through him. In that first class, he channelled the Archangel Mickhael, who spoke to us and offered to answer questions.

On getting the opportunity, I asked. "Who is the black horseman?"

After a short pause the answer came. *"The black horseman is you in another life."*

"Thank you. Can you tell me how and why I had that experience?"

There was another short pause. *"Jesus crossed your time lines to arouse your curiosity and to set you on your path."*

"Thank you." I was quietly confused and still wondering why these things were happening to me but the crossed time lines made sense. I asked another question, "Why did I have those visions of Jesus?"

"Jesus says that you were buried too deeply in the physical and he came to you in the manner he did to shock you. He says you were due to awaken at the age of fifty-five and as you have hidden yourself so deeply in the physical realm, it is necessary to begin now."

I didn't understand why Jesus was paying attention to me. I asked another question. "Can you tell me what the tangled part in the middle of my lifeline means?"

"Yes. It means that you will live through a time of tumultuous confusion."

"Thank you. May I ask another question?

"Yes, of course."

"In the vision I had early on New Year's Day, can you tell me what the golden face represented?"

"The golden face is Christ."

"Thank you." I had to pause a moment to digest that.

Mickhael added. *"Jesus has something he wants to say to you. He says. 'A drop in the ocean of existence.' Do you understand?"*

"Yes." Internally, I knew he meant that the drop falls into the ocean of existence. I suddenly realised that the ocean of existence was God.

Mickhael told me. *"There is more. He says. 'A mere drop in the ocean of existence.' Do you understand?"*

"Yes. Thank you. May I ask one more question?"

"Yes, my son."

"The extent of my injuries from the accident puzzled me. I was looking back at the injuries and I couldn't find anything that wasn't from the initial impact of when I went through the window and slapped into the ground. How is that possible when my car rolled several more times?"

"The three that were with you, that you saw as beings of light—Jesus, Uriel and another—wrapped themselves around you to prevent any further damage to your body."

"Thank you."

A couple of days later, I found myself sitting on the couch, wondering how I could make sense of all this new information. After talking with Mickhael, so much had become clear but I still felt like I had a puzzle to piece together. I needed to somehow cement this new knowledge into my consciousness but it took time to accept it.

I considered living through a time of tumultuous confusion.

Oh goody! I think I'm in the middle of that so, hopefully, it won't last too long.

And Jesus said. "*A drop in the ocean of existence.*"

To me, that meant I was a drop in the ocean of existence. So, if existence is the ocean and I was the drop, which would mean that we are all drops in the ocean of existence, and therefore we are all equal. We're all drops, going home, returning to God in our individual ways. The drops come from that massive body of water, that ocean of existence, like rain comes from our oceans as condensation only to return to that ocean after having made a journey. We're all from the same thing; the same ocean, finding our way back home.

A '*mere*' drop in the ocean of existence.

A warning to watch my ego. I can do that.

The next piece of information was that Jesus had crossed my timelines, '*to arouse my curiosity and set me on my path.*'

He definitely aroused my curiosity and set me on a path. So, what path did he set me on?

I took off from that experience to chase the black horseman, who was me in another life. That meant I was looking for myself.

So Jesus crossed my timelines, aroused my curiosity and set me on the path of self-awareness, but I still had no idea how to go about it.

On the following Thursday night, Jayson conducted a guided meditation that was specifically designed to meet and to receive a gift from our sponsoring archangel.

While in meditation, a figure appeared before me and identified himself as the Archangel Uriel. He was a little taller than I was, wore a robe like a monk's and his wings were not showing. He held something out to me with both hands: a gift.

I looked down to see a leather-bound book the colour of blood. Tentatively, I took the book from his hands and opened it. From front to back, every page it contained was blank.

I asked Uriel. "What's supposed to go in the book?"

"Your experiences. Fill the pages with the things you see on your journey."

Totally confused, I closed the book and thanked him for his gift. I asked. *"Who would want to read about me? I'm just a bricklayer."*

He just smiled. *"It's your book. Fill the pages. Write what you see."*

And then he was gone.

It took me a long time to work out that the book was the vehicle I needed for my journey.

As I came out of the meditation, my mind was whirling. I had been told, again, to write a book.

You have got to be kidding. I don't know anything about writing a book.

I was afraid and it was something else to bury at the back of my mind.

Part of the classes I attended focused on meditations designed for us to meet, get to know and be comfortable with our spirit guides. This time specifically, it was to be with our highest spirit guide, those known as our gatekeepers.

These are guides who stay with us for our entire lives. I was told that others come, do their job, and move on but these guys have us under their wings, so to speak, for our entire lives. It sounded a lot like the Christian concept of guardian angels to me.

In the meditation, I was guided to a clearing in a forest where, I was told if I was ready, he would come.

Jayson was good at taking people through guided meditations. I enjoyed the feel and smell of the forest while wondering what sort of experiences the other class members were having. As I wondered about theirs, I felt sure I wouldn't experience anything worth discussing.

I entered the forest clearing and found Jesus sitting on a log waiting for me. He was dressed in a long sleeved, off white robe belted at the waist. I didn't know how, but I knew that his robe was made from woven goat hair, that it was a working-man's robe. He wore leather sandals that wrapped several times around the ankles and calves; and I wore exactly the same robe and sandals as Jesus. Only I was a small child, maybe six years old, standing as high as the middle of his thigh; and I looked like a child playing dress-up wearing his much-too-big father's clothes.

I sat down beside him on the log in the middle of the forest clearing. I looked up and asked. "Why are you here?"

He looked down at me with laughter in his eyes. *"Write your book. All the answers are in it."*

He let me think about that for a bit and then said. *"I have been with you always, and I will be with you always. I am always with you. I do not want you to follow me, nor will I follow you, although I will always walk beside you. I will teach you through visions and dreams, through meditations like this one, and through astral travel. Put the things that you see into your book. As you write, the answers you seek will come to you. For now, take my hand and walk with me."*

Jesus reached his hand out to mine and we began walking across the clearing. I walked beside Jesus, hand in hand. With every step, I grew a little, and as we walked, I grew to adulthood. Our feet left the ground and we flew above the forest, our forms drifting together until there was only one; there was nothing separating us.

An Archangel's Gift

We flew down toward the forest stream, entered it, and became one with the water.

As water, we tickled lazy trout, gurgled happily over stones and drifted across pools until the roots of thirsty trees gathered us up. We became one with the trees. We became the forest. Squirrels, birds and butterflies played in our branches. We became water again and traveled through the trees, out through the leaves and were carried up to form clouds in the sky above the forest. As clouds the wind blew us toward the mountains where we fell as rain.

As water, we seeped into the mountain and once inside, we became the mountain. As the mountain, we looked out at the landscape below. We watched a forest grow where there was no forest before. We watched the forest grow old and turn to desert. We watched humankind come and build civilisations and be blown away by the sands of time. Then we left the mountain and came back down to the forest clearing.

As we approached the clearing, our forms separated.

Jesus turned to me. *"Do you understand?"*

"Yes, you have shown me everything is connected."

Now it was my turn to ask Jesus a question. "How long will it take me to write my book?"

"At least ten years."

"Thank you."

"Remember always, my son, everything is connected."

Then he was gone and I was back in class, no longer wondering what sort of experience anybody else had

An Archangel's Gift

Chapter 6

I Will Fight No More Forever

I was starting to feel trapped by my experiences and like I had no choice, so I fought the idea of writing a book and forgot the message Jesus had given me. I thought that if I just ignored the idea, it would go away.

I was also afraid of what people might think of me. In my mind, there was no way I was going to put what was happening to me in a book.

Shit! People might read it; then I'd get locked up for sure.

Regardless, I argued with myself. At least I thought it was me. I kept hearing. *"Write your book. Write your book."*

"I can't write a book. I don't know anything about writing books."

"Write your book."

"Why would I want to write a book?"

"Write your book; all the answers are in it."

"Shit! How do I write a book?"

"See, touch, feel, apply, know."

An Archangel's Gift

During a lull in the argument on a quiet spring morning, I was lazing about in my lounge room just staring out the window, quietly engrossed in the play of sunlight amongst the leaves of the chestnut tree when a vision unfolded before my eyes. Tears ran down my face and my throat constricted with emotion as I tried to understand what I was seeing.

But I didn't just see it. I could smell it, hear it and taste it on the air. All of my senses were engaged as war raged before me. The stench of rotting corpses, explosives and exhaust fumes mixed with that of the freshly killed and the sweet smell of newly turned earth filled my nostrils.

I saw a battlefield where men and women strove back and forth across the wounded and bleeding land, each seeking victory over the other at any cost. The noise of the battle was overpowering, for there were all the modern war machines playing their part. Small arms fire, machine guns, cannon, tanks, planes, helicopters and more, all unleashed their particular form of death, all added to the cacophony.

Slowly, I became more aware of other aspects of my surroundings. The battle turned, and I saw fresh and rotting carcasses of what had once been beautiful human beings.

I was looking over a landscape that resembled a garbage dump strewn with torn humanity when, I was chilled. Something was different; something else was happening.

A hush settled over the battlefield.

Men and women all over the field looked about them.

Even the wounded were silent. It was as though time froze while in the centre of the vision, a mist softly thickened. A shadow moved. Slowly, steadily, the shadow took form and a Native American warrior walked out of the past right onto the field of battle.

Waist length black hair billowed in a wind that wasn't there. From each temple hung a plait decorated with a single eagle feather. He wore buckskin leggings and breechcloth but nothing above the waist and his skin was tanned dark from the sun. No matter where people were on the battlefield, they could see him as he walked out of the obscuring mists of time and into view.

He seemed no more than thirty paces away, yet at the same time it felt as though he was thousands of miles and hundreds of years beyond this field. Blood seeped from minor wounds on his arms and chest. There were old scars on his body and I could tell by his clothes and weapons that he belonged to a time long past.

He strode to a small rise, in his left hand there was a knife covered with fresh blood. In his right hand he carried his fighting axe. On the head was fresh blood and pearl white chips of bone.

As he reached the top of the rise, he bent and laid his weapons on the ground at his feet. He put his hands in the blood of man and Mother Earth, then stood and faced the sun. He crossed his arms and placed a palm on each breast—left on right and right on left—leaving two handprints. He then drew the three middle fingers of his right hand, covered in mud and blood, from forehead to chin drawing three parallel lines down the centre of his face.

The warrior raised his eyes to the sky, and spreading his arms wide with his palms up and at shoulder height; he spoke his truth in a strong clear voice. "I will fight no more forever."

As the vision faded, I grabbed a pen and paper and struggled to write down what I had just seen. Tears fell onto the paper making it difficult to write, and it was hard to see as sobs continued to wrack my body.

For a long time, I agonised about using the warrior's quote because it was too close to that of Chief Joseph of the Nez Perce who fought a retreating action with his people against the U.S. Army in 1887. They fought for over three months and covered 1,170 miles (1,900kms) before surrendering and they fought with everything they had.

Then I realised that it was because they were Chief Joseph's words that they were so powerful. The vision was telling me that I would fight what was happening to me with everything I had. That I would fight until I had nothing left to fight with. Chief Joseph also used the words that were spoken by the warrior who stepped out of the mists of time in his surrender speech and they told me that I too would surrender in time.

The vision also told me that at some time in my future, an aspect of my past, would step into my future present.

An Archangel's Gift

Chapter 7

Follow the Earthen Cascade

I was at home trying to figure out what was happening to me, when another vision came.

I was standing in the yard of a run down, weatherboard, country house with two other people. The house, although the paint was peeling, the windows were broken, and the door hung ajar, was repairable. The two people with me were a young woman dressed in red and an old man with wrinkled, leathery skin. The woman's dress was made from a soft stretch fabric that hugged the contours of her body; it had a modern cut, short sleeves, a modest neckline, and it came to about mid-thigh. Her skin was golden brown, her eyes blue, and her auburn hair hung just past her shoulders and she was without shoes.

The old man was wearing black trousers and a shirt of medieval cut, he wore leather boots, a leather jerkin and scull-cap, these were all dark brown and yet lighter than his wrinkled skin. His apparel and appearance gave the impression of great age and yet he exuded strength, confidence and vitality. His eyes were dark brown and clear; his black hair came down to his shoulder blades and, even though I knew instinctively he was very old, there was no sign of grey in his hair.

The three of us stood on dry, hard packed ground where only a few stunted weeds grew.

We were between the house and a fence made up of Y-shaped black steel posts and five loosely strung wires. The barbed wire that should have been on the top was noticeably missing. It wasn't a very good fence and didn't look as though it could keep anything in or out.

I stood at the front of the house, halfway between it and the fence. The woman stood about thirty feet away, beside the fence. The old man was halfway between the house and fence and about halfway between me and the woman in red.

Immediately beyond the fence was a thick fog that obscured everything beyond it.

A very large black ant, about the same length as I was tall, dressed in a cream cricket blazer and wrap-around sunglasses, came out of the back door of the house and approached us.

At the same time as the ant stepped out of the door of the house, the woman leant down beside the fence, reached through and drew a red, leather bound book out from beneath a rock that had just a small corner poking through the fence.

She stood, opening the book. As she did, she gasped in surprise at what she saw, and said. "Come and look at this." The book she was holding in her hands was the same one Archangel Uriel had given to me.

The three of us came together and looked at the page of the book that had surprised her so much. At the same time the ant spoke. "Come with me. The bosses want to see you."

The ant then turned and retreated toward the house.

There on the page of the book was a drawing of the fence and the landscape beyond it that we couldn't see because of the fog. We looked at the drawing, then up at the fence and the fog, but the fog was gone and with that the whole rock that had been hiding the book was exposed. The rock was dark grey, a bit lumpy but smooth, about three feet long, one and a half feet high at its highest, and was covered in a scattering of washed out green spots of lichen. It sat like a sentinel at the beginning of a defined dirt path that led in a straight line, diagonally across level land carpeted in thick green grass. It led to an inviting and mysterious forest about fifty yards away. Purple wildflowers were scattered amongst the grass and I could see them crowding around the edge of the path as it followed the same line deep into the forest that was filled with dappled light and soft friendly shadows.

The drawing matched the landscape I was looking at, and beneath the drawing there was a caption written in italics.

Follow the Earthen Cascade by Edward Spellman, 2016.

I was standing directly in the line of the path so I could see down its unobstructed length deep into the forest.

The ant had expected us to follow it back into the house but the three of us moved toward the fence, where the path began beside the rock. I put my left foot on the bottom three wires pushing them to the ground and lifted the others, allowing my companions to slip through, and then I stepped through putting my right foot on the path beside the rock and quickly followed. We moved confidently along the newly exposed path as the vision faded, leaving me a bit stunned.

It took me almost twenty years to understand that the vision represented more than twenty years of my life.

The position I was standing in at the beginning of the vision represented me looking into my life or, my journey into self-awareness. I was standing between the run down house, my physical self, and my fears and doubts that kept me fenced in.

The hard packed ground I stood upon represented the difficulty in cultivating, or accepting, a healthy level of self, and spiritual, awareness.

I worked out most of the vision myself but had to get some help from Mickhael with the identity of the woman and the old man.

As I watched the vision, the woman in red, my *anima* or female aspect, reached under the rock and drew out this book. The rock represented the place in the back of my mind where I would hide all of those things I would rather not share. She opened the book to the page with the drawing captioned in italics. This pointed out that both the drawing and the caption were of paramount importance. That she wore no shoes connected her with nature.

The old man in the vision was ancient wisdom, and he represented the collective wisdom and knowledge of all of my souls' incarnations. He came along with me on my journey beyond the fence once the book was complete.

Once I began to question the meaning of the fog, I was stumped. I couldn't work it out.

Fog, fog, what is the fog?

As soon as I asked the question, the image I had been holding in my mind was moved aside and another replaced it. I was looking at the shadow of the warrior as he walked out of the mist and onto the battlefield.

What did the warrior have to do with the fog?

The fog came back, then the warrior in the mist, and I hear. *"No. Look."*

I saw the warrior again, walking out of the mist onto the field of battle.

As the two visions alternated and I tried to understand what I was shown, I heard. *"Remember always, my son, everything is connected."*

Then it clicked.

"It's not the warrior you're showing me, is it? It's the mist, the mists of time?"

It wasn't a fog at all.

I felt an energy wash over and through me. I felt it wash through my body, starting at the crown of my head and flowing right through to my feet. Somehow I knew it was Jesus telling me I had it right.

The giant ant was my ego and wearing a cricket blazer reinforced its desire to be one of the team. The recommendation was not to follow my ego but take an alternative path.

When it came to looking at the rock, the vision of my lifeline came and sat directly over this vision. The squiggly part of the lifeline vision that represented tumultuous confusion lined up with the rock from under which the book was drawn showing me that writing the book would be my time of tumultuous confusion. Also, the part of my lifeline that showed a new direction was in alignment with the path that began next to the rock, illustrating the new direction to come once the book was complete.

As the woman in red drew the book out, I saw that it was the same book Uriel gave me, and it was the same colour as the red leaves. Those red leaves were this book, which meant it already resided within my DNA. And the book was made up of the things I didn't want to share, so seeing visions and writing about them was in my DNA.

The caption, *Follow the earthen cascade,* was of paramount importance because I could read it clearly. As I asked myself, what is an earthen cascade? I saw a vision of a landslide, which made sense. A landslide was earth cascading in a way.

What did a landslide do?

It removed all obstacles from its path and exposed what was underneath.

That meant that writing this book would help remove all the obstacles I would likely put in front of myself, and expose my inner self. If the obstacles were removed, opportunities would flow. The drawing showed that once the book was complete, my path, once having moved beyond my fears and doubts, would be smooth and unobstructed.

Stepping onto the path with my right foot meant that I should be sure to undertake this journey, to walk this path, with the *right* intention.

Being able to see down the length of the path told me that after I stepped through the fence, there would be no obstacles. The path being clearly defined told me that my own path would be the same.

In the vision, three aspects of self came together, rejected the advice of the ego, and moved off in a completely different direction.

Chapter 8
Running Wolf

After seeing the warrior again, I thought I would try to find out who he was.

I put on some incense and got comfortable in my lounge room, and with some soft music in the background, I drifted off into meditation asking. "Who is the warrior I saw walking out of the mists of time?"

The speed of the reply surprised me, as I hadn't really expected one.

"He is Running Wolf of the Bear Clan of the Sioux Nation."

I got myself a pen and paper and wrote that down then wandered about the house for a while. I had a cup of tea that I didn't finish, and wandered about a bit more wondering if I could find out more.

I decided to meditate again and look for him with more focus.

An Archangel's Gift

I got myself comfortable and watched as the morning sunlight glistened on dewdrops amongst my slightly overgrown garden. I didn't have the heart to cut back the plants.

Small clouds drifted by as I took a deep cleansing breath, closed my eyes, and visualised myself walking through a deep red mist. I inhaled the mist slowly, deeply, and exhaled as I walked up a flight of steps while still in the mist. At the top of the steps was a landing, and the mist changed to orange. I took another deep breath and moved to the next flight of steps. I exhaled as I walked up the steps to a second landing and another color change, this time to yellow. I inhaled and moved forward, then exhaled and walked up the stairs. At the next landing the colour was forest green and I inhaled that into my body and moved forward. Again I exhaled and moved up the stairs to where the colour changed to sky blue. I inhaled sky blue and moved forward, exhaled and walked up the next flight where the colour changed to indigo. I breathed deeply of the indigo mist and moved across the landing to the next flight of steps, exhaling as I walked up them.

As I stepped onto the final landing, the colour changed to white with pink flecks. I breathed that deeply into my lungs as time and space dissolved into a mist.

I was looking at a camp from above and a little to the side, as if I was watching from the basket of a hot air balloon tethered above the camp.

I saw three people going about their daily chores: Running Wolf, his wife and their son.

They had their lodge at the edge of a small clearing on the high side of a river, and there was an outside cooking fire with meat drying on racks.

There were elk, cougar and muskrat skins stretched on frames to dry in the sun.

Two horses were hobbled close by, enjoying the fresh spring grass.

A flintlock rifle leant against a tree close to where he was working on a fresh elk hide. He had a powder horn and a shot pouch slung across his body.

To the left of the entrance of the lodge leant a war lance; it stood as tall as he could reach and had a blade as wide as his hand and two hands in length. On the right side of the entrance a buffalo bow hung with a quiver full of arrows.

The mist that had cleared to open that window in time and place drifted back and soon all I could see was mist. I took a deep breath, wiggled my toes and fingers, and then slowly opened my eyes to find myself back in my lounge room.

An Archangel's Gift

Chapter 9
The Horseman Again

Having found Running Wolf a couple of days earlier, I started to wonder if I could do the same thing with the black horseman.

The horseman fascinated me, so I was going to see if I could find him too. I found a comfortable position, drew in a breath to centre myself, and called to my guides for protection.

I visualised myself climbing a stair shrouded in red mist, as I moved upward the colours changed. Red to orange, orange to yellow, slowly I moved deeper into myself. Yellow to green, and up to blue, I felt the blood pumping through my veins. Blue to indigo, and then I climbed the stair to a platform bathed in pure white light with pink flecks.

Jesus was waiting for me, a half smile on his lips and dressed in clothes similar to those of the horseman and his friends. He knew what I was after. On the other side of the platform stood a door; we approached it together and walked through. There was another stairway before us, which we began to climb side by side.

As we climbed higher, our forms moved together until there was only one figure climbing the stairs.

We climbed higher and our form blended into the mists of time and space, and we drifted into the past.

Coming out of the mist, I felt really strange. It was like I was watching the horseman from a distance, and also looking through his eyes. The way words formed in my mind twisted and changed as though there were the two of us in the same mind.

I saw him riding across the countryside with a woman. It didn't seem very purposeful as they just dawdled along, stopping every now and then to have something to eat, to rest the horses and enjoy the day.

Then the scene changed and the horseman was alone in a forest at the base of a cliff.

He sat astride one of the best trained warhorses that land, or any, had seen for many a year: a horse that men would kill for, and he was about to abandon him to the fates.

They had bled together before that day, and if the Goddess willed, would have the chance to do so again. Merely fifty paces in front of him stood a cliff that stretched to each side as far as the eye could see, and whose top was shrouded in mist. That cliff looked like it thought it could not be climbed; it sat there and mocked any who would dare try.

It was, for the black horseman however, the way he had to go and no other. He laughed at the misconceptions of the cliff and went about his preparations.

For three days he had traveled through the forest to come to this place. There was a clearing with plenty of grass and a small stream to one side. He stripped the horse of his gear and hid it close by in the forest, in the bowl of an oak tree.

He was dressed only in dark homespun wool and black leather, his armour being too cumbersome for the task. A pair of swords was strapped to his shoulders and a strong fighting knife with an eight-inch blade rested at the small of his back. The swords he carried were twins, both with a blade the length of his arm; they were simple weapons with silver hilt and guard, unadorned with a two-inch silver sphere atop the hilt. A poor man's swords they seemed at first sight, but they were a gift from his father's people and there were few finer.

The horse would not stray until the food ran out, and if he was not back by that time, he would be dead.

He strode toward the black cliff face, whistling a tune from his boyhood.

Other than the swords and knife, he carried only bread and cheese in a pouch slung over one shoulder and a small water-skin over the other.

An Archangel's Gift

An ancient oak leant against the cliff face, blown over in some past storm; it would get him part way up.

Up into the mist he climbed, unable to see how far to the top. Stop and rest, climb again, mist billowing about him. After some hours, he climbed out of the mist and onto the cliff top; the forest came right up to the edge.

Late in the afternoon, he found what he was looking for: a small lake with an island in the centre. On that island was a fortified stone house with gardens at the back.

The path to the house, known as the 'sword's edge' ran across the lake but was hidden beneath the water's surface and very narrow so only one horse could cross at a time. It was well known that *'dragon's teeth'* also guarded this place, a ring of cruel spikes that circled the island hidden beneath the water's surface.

To walk the sword's edge was to die, as it was guarded at all times by archers so his only chance to get onto the island unseen was to swim at night and risk the dragon's teeth.

He waited until dark and walked out as far as he could, then swimming slowly, inch by inch, until he found the first of those dragon's teeth. His chest had run into it, causing a scratch and giving him a warning. There were six rows of the dragon's teeth to pass.

Once onto the island, he emerged scratched on his arms and legs but still moved stealthily to a small door at the back, where the inhabitants came to pick fresh vegetables from the garden.

He set himself beside the door and waited for the morning.

Up to that point of the meditation, I thought I was simply an invisible passenger but when it was almost dawn, he asked me not to accompany him, as I would be too distracting and he would have to fight once inside.

I withdrew my awareness as someone lifted the bar to the iron bound oak door and a heavyset man carrying a basket appeared.

The horseman made one quick knife thrust, was through the door and closed it behind him.

Time passed and I wondered what was happening inside. I moved my awareness around to the front of the house and back to the other side of the lake so I could watch the front door until he passed through the front gate on horseback. Another horse followed, carrying the woman he came to rescue. Somehow I knew that she was his cousin, the same woman I had seen him with earlier.

The horses knew the path and walked it confidently.

Before they reached the shore of the lake, my vision clouded and I felt myself drifting back into my body. I took a deep breath, moved my fingers, wriggled my toes and opened my eyes. That was my black horseman: me in a past life.

An Archangel's Gift

As I sat contemplating what I just experienced and without any intent on my part, I found myself again with the horseman, although this time it was the reverse of what happened in Cooma. It was the horseman looking through my eyes at the Cooma streets.

Spring sunshine filled the countryside around me, a gentle breeze moved the knee length grass, kissed the new growth on the ancient oaks.

My stallion flexed his muscles beneath me; I felt his chest expand as he inhaled. He snorted, pulled at the reins and stamped, eager to be off.

Then it was as though I sat inside a strange carriage, yet no horses did I see. It moved along as though by magick and strange houses did I pass. The carriage moved along a black road with white stripes at its centre.

I saw tall, straight poles with ropes strung between, what use could they possibly be? No walls, nor battlements nor towers; this must be a peaceful place for it could not be defended.

I had just experienced how the horseman experienced Jesus crossing our timelines. He thought he was looking into another realm, the realm of the Fae.

He was experiencing driving on a bitumen road in a four wheel drive, looking out at suburban Australia along a street lined with telephone poles, while sitting on a horse about fifteen-hundred years ago.

That felt even stranger than the first time it happened, sort of like time travel into someone else's body, and like someone else was having the same experience and we were both aware of the other.

Yet again I had to ask myself. *Why is this stuff happening to me?*

An Archangel's Gift

Chapter 10
The Negative Aspects of Self

My experiences were on my mind when I woke up each morning, and they were there as I went to sleep. I was drifting between having fun with them and worrying about my sanity.

One morning, I was lying in bed at dawn and as I stared at the ceiling, my vision fogged. The world swirled and I found myself walking through a belt of grassland with a crooked staff in my hand between two lots of pine trees. The staff was decorated with crystals and carved with runes. I didn't understand why I would have a staff like that, but it felt right.

I walked through the grass and came across a pool of water. The surface of the pool was calm and still with sunlight hitting it in such a way that I could not see beneath the surface.

Although I had seen pools of water before, this one came with the knowledge that it represented something quite unfamiliar to me.

I stood beside the pool and only saw reflections, so I reached out the staff and slid it beneath the surface of the water. I then saw clearly beneath the surface and I was back in my bed again, staring at the ceiling.

I realised I had been asking what was happening to me and why I was having these experiences and here I was shown that I could see below the surface.

What surface?

Oh! The earthen cascade…the landslide exposed what was hidden beneath the surface…my surface. The vision told me that the process was exposing and experiencing parts of myself that I was unaware of.

Alongside this understanding, I was coming to terms with the idea of writing a book so I meditated and asked my guides to show me what I needed to learn.

As my consciousness moved deeper into meditation, I found myself driving through the countryside. The landscape was flat and sandy with a sparse covering of eucalypts.

As I approached my destination—a large, green farm shed—I was the last to arrive as several cars were already parked there, close to the shed and a levee bank.

I parked and entered the shed through a large door at the centre. It smelled new and looked as though it had only just been built.

Once inside, I saw that the floor was not concrete as I expected but soft, red desert sand. There were footprints all over the place but the people that had been there had already left.

As I looked around, the woman in the red dress arrived; my anima. We began looking for the others and eventually we stood at the top of the levee bank looking over to the other side where there were six bodies lying on the ground. Somehow I knew these were the people who had been in the shed.

Together we went down and built a pyre for the bodies, which we then collected and set on top. As I stood looking down at them, a lighted torch in my hand, I realised that the bodies were all negative aspects of myself.

The woman in the red dress and I thrust our burning torches into the pyre, setting it ablaze. As the fire took hold, we moved to the top of the levee to watch.

Hand in hand, we looked into the roaring flames and said. "We ask the Creator to take these negative aspects of our self into the Light as we cannot use them anymore; we deliver them up to You."

As we watched, the burning pyre burst into a whirlwind of fire. Inside the whirlwind there were printed pages, pages I had written and would write; burning as they floated upwards and within minutes, all were consumed.

Soon green shoots began to push through the previously barren soil toward the beckoning sky. Within minutes, a grove of mature trees stood where the pyre had roared moments before. As the trees reached their full growth, our bodies flowed together to become once again, simply, myself.

And so I learnt that was how I would start writing a book. First, I needed to get the rubbish out of my head. The vision told me to write from the negative to get all of it out, and then burn it to release myself from the negative critic inside myself. That opened up space for my creative self to write what I needed to write.

The empty shed was me. With the negative gone, I knew it was waiting to be filled with the positive.

Chapter 11
Teacher

I kept coming across the concept of a teacher coming into the world in the end of days to show us the way. I began to wonder if that meant, *the way to self and spiritual awareness.*

In my reading, the teacher concept appeared in most religions, which fanned my curiosity and I wondered if I could find him or her in the same way I found Running Wolf and the black horseman.

I set myself up in a comfortable spot, drifted into meditation and heard these words. *"He who walks in the Light."*

These words repeated themselves until I wrote them down and as soon as I had, I heard another set, which I wrote down.

Then it happened again, and again, and again.
This is what I heard.

An Archangel's Gift

He who walks in the Light
And does so with humility
May pass where others may not

The teacher will be ridiculed
His books will be torn and burnt
Few shall see the truth
Though on the day the world is torn
Realisation will dawn like a rising sun

Then his words will be sought
And with fear in their hearts
They will try to raise him over others

A wave of fear will run
Through the hosts of man
When they think the end has come
Once more they will look at prophecy
And grasp whatever they can

False prophets there will be at every turn
Proclaiming to all
"Salvation is yours if you but follow me"
Beware! For they preach the defiled word
Yet believe in every one

Edward Spellman

If they preach not harmony
And goodwill to all
Have a care to whom you listen
For though prophet they may claim to be
There is not one truth that suits all men and women but that,
ALL, are equal in the eyes of Divinity

Take care, for those that give you pretty words
May not be all they claim
The teacher comes believe or not
He walks amongst you now
He treads his path in silence
And walks amongst the crowds

Be humble before your maker
And live your life
In a way that makes you proud

To seek the messenger is humanity's nature
Though when you find him
Place him not upon a pedestal
For then the message will be lost

Remember now if he says
I am the teacher
You can be sure he's not the one

An Archangel's Gift

The one you seek will teach forbearance
And the interconnection of all life
He will speak of harmony and equality
Yet will not preach a word

A tradesman's hands
And a humble heart
Are all he has to offer

If at first you find false prophets
Take heart and look again
For if there is to be a teacher
There will be many that claim they are he

Their miracles will be manifold
Their appearance Divine
For the false prophet needs his miracles
To announce his place in the world

Fear not if you find one
For their very existence
On this world and at this time
Proves that there is a teacher

Edward Spellman

A true prophet needs no fanfare
And he is the one they fear
For his truth will leave them powerless
And the Truth shall set you free.

That made me nervous. Here was something I would have preferred to leave hidden under the rock in the back of my mind, which is exactly why I left it in…because it made me uncomfortable.

I sat for a while, absorbing what I had heard, then got up and as I walked across the lounge room, I saw another vision. It was so strong that the impact caused me to forget where I was going.

A huge earthquake shattered the world around me, followed by a monstrous tidal wave that inundated the entire landscape and washed everything clean. The waters soon receded leaving fertile soil and seeds carried from far away. Shoots began to push through the soil and in a short time, there was a verdant forest where moments before there was only desert.

I found it intensely emotional, as it told me that if I continued along the path into self-awareness, my perceptions of myself and my reality would be shattered as is shown by the earthquake.

It told me that if I continued along that path, I would be cleansed and healed, as symbolised by the salt water in the tidal wave.

An Archangel's Gift

And it told me that once the shattering of my world and healing occurred, my perceptions of self and the world would be renewed, as shown by the new growth of the forest.

Just as I finished writing down the vision of earthquakes and tidal waves, and with my pen still in my hand, I saw another.

I was standing on a high plain where the colours were brighter and the air clearer than what I usually saw. In the distance, a dense, lush forest stood. Before me, a massive stone building was at the centre of a raised stone platform with seven steps running continuously all around it.

I approached the platform and climbed the steps up to the building. Then I walked around the entire structure and found no windows or doors.

The building was made of large blocks of unadorned, dressed stone and was set out as an equal armed cross. Each of the four wings had an identical barrel vaulted roof that overhung the walls by about half a metre, forming an upward curving eave.

From where the four wings converged, a circular tower rose to about half the height again of the rest of the building.

Having found no entrance, I imagined myself inside, and suddenly, I was. The inside of the building was lit from an unseen source and both the walls and floor were finished in polished green Aventurine.

Then I was back in my house again, pen still in my hand.

On asking Mickhael about the building, he told me it was the Repository of Knowledge, and that it existed within an alternate reality.

The rest I worked out for myself. The building had no windows or doors because it exists as part of the inner self, so to access it, I needed to undertake a journey into self-awareness.

I came to understand that it is accessible when the student reaches a specific level of self-awareness and spiritual maturity.

Aventurine is the stone of opportunity, and that told me my path would create opportunities as I progressed.

An Archangel's Gift

Chapter 12

Success

One quiet morning, I had just been poking around doing some housework when another vision appeared. It was hard to describe because it had two separate parts that overlapped in the centre.

Spread out across the landscape before me was a strange vision of war on one side, and the clear felling of a forest on the other.

On the left side was the clear felled forest, where the trees were being cut down. As I watched, men and machines cut down and destroyed everything. To the right, I saw warfare where men and women were being cut down.

When I looked to the centre of the vision, it was really hard to focus and I found that part impossible to describe. I couldn't see where one part of the vision ended and the other began. It was as though two dimensions or realities converged and interacted in such a way as to make it impossible to tell which was which. It was chaos.

An Archangel's Gift

Although being virtually impossible to describe, the difficulty it presented showed me how to interpret the vision. It meant that, on a spiritual level, there was no difference between cutting down a fellow man or woman, or clear felling a forest. It meant that, as we have a soul, so too does the forest.

As I tried to absorb what I had seen, I got hit with another vision, almost before I could draw breath. I saw myself standing on a ledge halfway up a cliff that was several hundred feet high. I stood there facing a wall of stone that completely blocked my path.

The ledge was about six feet wide so there was no danger of falling off, although as I looked to my right and left, I noticed that it did not go very far in either direction and the stone was smooth and hard. There were no cracks or openings that would allow me to climb either up or down.

Beside me on the ground was a supply of miners hand tools.

As I looked at the cliff face in front me, I asked myself what it represented and I knew the answer. This was the task ahead.

Then, standing in that place where I couldn't go left, right, up, down or back, I had two choices. I could sit and do nothing or I could take up the tools I was supplied with and cut my way forward. If I sat there and did nothing, I knew I would wither and die. I took up the tools and marked the cliff in the shape and size of a standard household doorway.

As I cut through the stone, I took care to keep the walls, ceiling and floor of the tunnel straight and smooth with the corners neat and finely detailed.

I dug, focused on my task until my chisel broke through the other side. I stopped for a little while, amazed to see how far I had come, then carefully finished my tunnel.

As I stood at the end of the tunnel, it felt like a doorway to another world. I looked out onto a world where the air was clearer, the sky was bluer, and the trees and the grass were greener. I took a deep breath of that *magickal* air and was back in my house again wondering what I had been doing before the vision came.

I understood I had just received more advice about my book and the journey. The vision told me that if I wanted to succeed, there was really no choice but to move forward and that if I kept my focus and used the tools I had at hand, I would make my way through all the difficulties into a world that would be much more than the one I inhabited.

An Archangel's Gift

Chapter 13
The Devil's Waiting Room

In my dreams and meditations and everywhere I turned, I was given the book; this book, again and again and again. The cover was the colour of blood and all the pages were blank.

Again, I asked Uriel. "Why is the book blank? What's supposed to go in it?"

The answer was always the same. *"Fill the book with the things that you see. Fill it with your story. At this time that is your task."*

But I still didn't understand why anyone would be interested in my dreams, meditations and visions. And I was afraid. Fear is a powerful weapon and a worthy adversary, and I was learning that it was only there to be overcome.

I also kept fighting with Jesus.

In my mind, I stamped my foot and screamed. *I can't do this.* While all the time, I really, really wanted to.

Why me?

"Because you are in the right place, my son."

What the hell does that mean?

Sometimes the whole thing really pissed me off and I wanted him gone from my life. He told me some time ago that this would happen and together we designed a visualisation for me when I felt angry, frustrated or afraid. The visualisation was of Jesus wearing a robe and sandals, hefting a two-foot long fresh fish, which he proceeded to hit me with on the side of my head. We borrowed this scenario from a Monty Python skit in one of their movies except that in the movie it was John Cleese with the fish, not Jesus.

So I fought, and screamed. I stamped my foot and swore and out came the fish and I would burst out laughing at Jesus slapping me in the head with a large wet one. It worked every time but I still tended, occasionally, to do something that required the wet fish treatment.

Maybe I really would just keep fighting until I had no fight left.

Even though I kept arguing with him, I knew that ultimately he was doing, or guiding me toward, the thing or things and experiences that were inevitably in my best interest.

So how long will I keep up the fight? I wondered.

In my dreams I was asked by Archangel Uriel to do him a favour.

Of course, anything.

"Write your book. Fill the pages with the things you see."

This was all so far beyond the borders of my perceptions of reality that to help myself deal with the visions and the interactions with Jesus, I had to water it down for myself and talk about them as if they were everyday occurrences, and as if he was just another friend. If I were to look at the enormity of what was happening to me, I couldn't handle it.

I had a shed in my backyard that I had set up as a little leather workshop. I'd been working on a shoulder bag and was just standing, staring out the window at the garden, allowing my mind to drift at the workbench.

My hands still held a needle and thread when I found myself in a room about ten paces' square. It felt like a waiting room, although a rather strange one. A mediocre artist had painted all four walls, ceiling and floor with flames.

There were no windows or doors except for a small silver door in the far wall that looked like the door to a furnace or kiln. It was about two feet high and eighteen inches wide. Facing the door were three rows of stools made from log offcuts and painted bright red with yellow tops.

An Archangel's Gift

The three rows of stools sat toward the back of the room facing the furnace door and I stood barefoot in front of the first row facing the door as well.

Although I didn't feel it, I knew the room was supposed to be intimidating.

The door slowly opened and waves of heat washed across the room: a disgusting sense of heat, not the clean heat of fire, but something terribly wrong.

Through the open door a grotesque, human-like face, on the end of a tentacle slid into the room. I knew somehow that this obscene thing with a face but no head to speak of was just a small part of the evil it represented.

The thing stopped a couple of feet into the room and stared at me. I could see hate, loathing, and a desire to inflict pain upon me. Strangely, even though it was trying to project these feelings onto me, I remained calm.

It moved closer and spoke, and as it spoke drops of acid dripped from its mouth and sizzled on the floor. It said. *"Ask for anything, anything and you can have it."*

Even though that was all it said, I knew that it was offering to fulfil anything I desired. I also knew the price. The price was everything, everything that I am; everything I could be, which included my soul.

I knew that this place was supposed to threaten me into making a mistake and asking for something but I was protected.

Again it hissed. *"Ask for anything."*

This time a question rose from the depths of my mind and I asked. "How many souls have to come to the Light to save humanity?"

My question made it angry and it tried to move further into the room but it was stopped somehow.

"How many souls have to come to the Light to save humanity?"

The entity grew angrier and again tried to come further into the room but again it was stopped.

"ASK."

This time there was a threat of retribution in the way it screamed at me, but none of it touched me.

For the third time, I asked. "How many souls have to come to the Light to save humanity?"

I saw hatred emanating from it because it knew it couldn't have me. It drew back like a snake about to strike and breathed fire directly at me.

I threw up my arms reflexively to protect my face although the flames never touched me. Fire roared into the room, but left me untouched. I lowered my arms and watched the flames stopped and turned aside by invisible shielding. I understood I was protected from everything the entity projected at me.

With the fire still roaring at me, I blinked my eyes and I was no longer in that room. I was standing in a mountain meadow under a summer sky with soft, fluffy clouds drifting by and golden sunshine caressing my body.

My bare feet teased by soft green grass; my choice was made.

Then I was back in my shed, my hands halfway through what they had been doing before.

Around this time, it seemed that as soon as one vision finished, another came and I was overwhelmed. I was suddenly in the middle of a stormy ocean with wave after wave crashing against me.

And again, almost before I had a chance to get my head around the last vision, another arrived.

Before me was a large swimming pool with many tennis balls being forced far beneath the water's surface. As I watched, the tennis balls were pushed deeper and deeper.

Soon I noticed some movement, some resistance to the controlling force, until one of the tennis balls broke free and leapt to the surface. The ball shot from the surface of the pool and fell back down to float in the sunlight.

Before long, other tennis balls broke free and leapt to the surface.

Then I was back, still staring out the window of my workshop.

It meant that there are parts of myself that I have repressed, forced down as hard as I could, and that the same force I used to push those parts down, is the force that will ultimately break them free.

That meant by trying my hardest *not to write* this book, I was generating the energy and motivation to do it.

An Archangel's Gift

Chapter 14
Wind Blows, Rivers Flow

I was sitting outside, enjoying the wind through the trees and thinking about how my priorities had changed since the car accident. My business had been going well before it and growing nicely. I was thinking about selling it and doing some travelling. Now my business didn't interest me at all.

As those thoughts drifted through my mind I saw a vision of an old fashioned wooden barrel of apples, and all of the apples were rotten.

A hand reached out and placed one ripe apple into the middle of the rotten ones in the barrel.

I watched as the rotten apples began to change. First the rotten apples that were touched by the ripe one ripened. Then the apples that touched those ripened until soon, there were no rotten apples left.

Argh! I don't want to know. I don't want to know. La, la, la, la, la.

I took a deep breath and stepped a little closer. I walked around the barrel, leaning in to see the apple that had been placed there. I poked it with my finger. What was it about that particular apple that affected me so strongly?

I wanted to be the ripe apple but it was really the barrel of rotten ones that represented me. I didn't want to be a barrel of rotten apples. I wanted to stamp my foot and say. *I want to be the ripe apple.*

What made it change?

What made me change?

Then I knew what the apple was: an idea, a concept, and a task. The apple was the process of becoming self-aware, and the hand that put it there belonged to Jesus.

Following their advice would lead to me being rejuvenated and renewed. I didn't know if that meant physically, spiritually, emotionally or all three, but I suddenly felt excited instead of scared.

Aside from the visions and dreams, there were also times when three or four words repeated themselves in my mind and the only way to stop them was to write them down. As soon as that was done, the next three or four words would come, and so it continued until whatever it was, was complete.

Two days after the vision of the apples, these words echoed through my mind. *Wind blows rivers flow, wind blows rivers flow; wind blows, rivers flow.*

Edward Spellman

    I knew that game well by then and knew the words would just repeat until I recorded them, so I began to write:

Wind blows, rivers flow.
Mountains rise, mountains fall.
Mankind crawls from the primal ooze
To stand upon the Earth.

Mankind rises, reaches for the stars, falls. Why?
Is he not made in the image of God?
Is he not made to rule the Earth?
Should not fall but continue to rise?

Mankind rises, and falls, again.
Puzzled, he wonders why.
Is he not made in the image of God?
Is He not, therefore, the ultimate being?

Should not fall but continue to rise?
Rise to be all-powerful.
Mankind rises. Falls, again.
Confused, he stops and looks about.

Mankind rises to rule the Earth.
Falls, again.
Is it truth, or is it not, was man not made to rule the Earth?

An Archangel's Gift

Mankind has a soul.
What of the birds, or the fish?
What of the rocks, the trees, the animals?
Do they, or do they not, have a soul?

In a universe as great and diverse as this, would you, if you were Creation, mold only one thing, with an immortal soul?
Think with your heart, not with your ego.

To my mind, from smallest to largest,
from animate to inanimate, all things created,
have a soul equal to our own.

Mankind rises. Mankind falls. Why?
Mankind falls, and rises again.
Is he master, is he slave, or is he partner in his destiny?

When the truth he accepts, no more shall he fall,
but come into his own.
Then shall he rise; no more shall he fall.

No more shall he war on the planet, his home.
But treat Her, with the respect, as our Mother, she deserves.

For rock and tree, man and planet, the sun and the stars, are all parts of a whole.

Edward Spellman

Our planet, Gaia, gives freely of her abundance.
With respect, we should take only that, which we need to survive.

Mankind rises, and hand in hand with the Earth, our home.
Will move forward, to fulfill our destiny.

After waiting for a couple of minutes to make sure the flow of words had stopped, I reread what I wrote.

I think stunned and flabbergasted are the right words for how I felt. I shook my head and wondered. *What the hell's going on with me?*

Just breathe.

An Archangel's Gift

Chapter 15
Edward

For a year, the group of people I met at Jayson's personal and psychic development classes got together at my place on Saturday nights, which often included channeled messages from Spirit.

One of the Saturday night channels with Jayson was interesting. But then again, they always were. The energy we met that night was from a recently deceased person, which was unusual. Just as unusual, it was from someone famous. The energy was female, and came to us a year after her death. As she spoke to each of us in turn she asked us to say our names. When it was my turn she asked. "What is your name?"

"Dush." I replied with my nickname. For most of my life I had refused to answer to anything else, especially my Christian name.

"I will not call you that. What were you christened?"

Reluctantly, I answered. "Edward."

"A royal name. I will call you Edward."

I got the distinct impression that she was happy that she had gotten me to acknowledge my name. As though it were something on her to do list that she could now cross off.

"Thank you."

That left me stunned and it felt like an important part of my journey into self-awareness, to stop denying my own name.

Never before had I allowed anyone to call me Edward, and yet all of a sudden, I liked it. It was as though I had only just realised that I was Edward, and Dush moved into the background.

In the middle of cooking my evening meal, I found myself walking through a mountain meadow, with a familiar staff in my right hand. I'd stuck it in a pool of water in another vision.

I came to a stone building which allowed me entry, as though it was expecting me. Inside were all sorts of useful items stacked upon shelves and packed in alcoves. There was a ground level set of rooms, a basement room, and a second level below the stone roof.

The entire building was a storeroom and somehow, without being told, I knew that everything in it was part of me and reflected what I was learning between my experiences and writing them into my book.

The vision told me that there was more to me than I knew and that if I continued, I would discover and uncover more than I could possibly imagine.

During another channelling session with Jayson, Jesus asked. *"Think about this. How would you feel if you had to carry everything you own on your back?"*

"Now think about this: how would you feel if you could carry everything you own on your back?"

Then he asked. *"What if this is all just boot camp?"*

If it is all just boot camp, I thought, *I'd love to know what the training was for.*

Nathan, one of the Saturday night regulars, decided that he was sick of Canberra and was going to move cities, probably to Sydney.

Within a couple of weeks, it had changed from one person moving to Sydney to six people moving to Melbourne. I was asked, along with my partner at the time, if we would join them.

"I can't move to Melbourne." I said. "I have a house, a mortgage and a business here. I can't afford to move."

After saying that I couldn't afford to move, I was asked. "What would happen if you went bankrupt?"

"I can't go bankrupt." I said, my ego kicking in to protect me.

But that question from one of my friends made me think. My house was mortgaged up to capacity as I had been living off the equity since the car accident when my business virtually died that same day. I still did a little work but truthfully I was not earning enough to pay the bills. When I did a financial projection of my business of glass brick installation, I could see that I would be bankrupt before the next year was out anyway.

After thinking about bankruptcy for a couple of days, I decide to talk to my accountant.

One and a half hours of both my accountant and her boss giving me a host of reasons why I should not go bankrupt and I was still not sure what to do. Should I go bankrupt or should I stay and try to work it out?

I went home and thought about it. I was lying on the brick paving of my BBQ area and staring at the clouds thinking about everything the accountants said. They encouraged me to get a second job and work, work, work: to do anything to avoid going bankrupt. The truth was that since the accident it usually took me about a week to recuperate from one day's work as it was. I didn't think I could handle a second job.

Then there were the visions and how I was promised a change of direction for the better after a time of tumultuous confusion.

Could a move to Melbourne be part of that?

The vision, *Follow the earthen cascade,* showed me that a new path would open for me after I finished the book, but Jesus told me that would take at least ten years.

Bummer.

In the vision, *I will fight no more forever,* it showed that an aspect of my past would step into my future present and that I would stop resisting my path.

As I thought, I was staring up at the clouds, watching their shapes: within the clouds I was watching a phoenix rose from the ashes and all my doubts about moving to Melbourne washed away.

I knew that somehow; I would rise from the ashes of my own destruction as did the phoenix.

I had also seen a premonition a couple of days earlier of myself if I stayed where I was and kept doing what I had been doing. In the premonition I was fat and crippled up with arthritis.

So! Bankruptcy it was.

An Archangel's Gift

Chapter 16
An Invitation

Our Saturday night channel came around again and my turn to ask Mickhael a question came. "Why do I have the ability to go back in time during meditation?"

"You have that ability so you can go back and check the details of the things you write about." came the simple reply. There was a short pause before he continued. *"Jesus has a favour to ask."*

I felt a rush of curious excitement at the request. "Yes, of course, anything."

"He asks that you go back and watch his crucifixion."

Internally I wasn't so sure I could do that, but I said, "I can do that." I could feel the hair standing up on the back of my neck as my mind screamed, *No, no, no, no, no!*

Jesus' request terrified me.

I knew that going back to watch Jesus' crucifixion was going to be a very painful thing for me to do. Even though I had said yes, I did not feel ready to face it.

An Archangel's Gift

Seeing as how I was moving to Melbourne and would no longer have access to Mum and Dad's farm, I camped out there for a few days before the big move. I went to meditate, at Jesus' request, by the oldest tree on the farm.

It was an ancient tree and I felt drawn to it, more so as he suggested that I sit with it and meditate.

I wondered, *what is he up to?*

Once at the farm, I camped in a place my family and I called Deer Valley, which was quite close to where the old tree was.

Early on the first morning there, I hiked up to the old tree, spread my poncho on the ground not far from it, and sat down to meditate.

While in meditation, I saw myself walking through the bush toward my camp with a crooked staff in hand. As I opened my eyes and blinked a couple of times, I saw right in front of me, the branch of the tree that would be the staff I saw in my hand while meditating.

Looking at the branch, which was really a trunk, as the tree was a species of mallee. It has multiple trunks and grows to only about four meters tall. I wondered why Jesus wanted me to have a staff from that particular tree?

I chose not to second guess my guidance and cut the staff. With deep gratitude, I thanked the tree for its gift and walked back to camp.

It was raining lightly and the wind was gusting and swirling about as I sat by my campfire and trimmed my new staff. I scraped off the bark while sitting in the wind and the rain. Once the bark was off, I ran the staff through the flames to dry it a little, then rubbed dirt all over it. My staff was born in earth, air, fire and water.

I wasn't sure how or why that was important but I was certain it was.

By Christmas, I was bankrupt and had sold almost everything I owned, raising enough money to move cities and start over.

My business wasn't saleable, as it had been losing money steadily since July '96. Car accidents and self-employment didn't seem to be compatible. I sold what gear I could for the move and worked out that I got around ten cents on the dollar for my furniture.

The vision of my lifeline gave me hope and drew me forward. Perhaps this was what it was all about.

An Archangel's Gift

Melbourne

1999 to 2005

An Archangel's Gift

Chapter 17
Bleeding Fingers

We made it to Melbourne and it was extraordinarily easy in the end to let everything go. I called the bank and told them that I could no longer cover my mortgage payments and posted them the keys to the house back in Canberra. All the while, there were visions, dreams and prophecies spinning around in my mind, all jumbled up. I needed space and I needed time to figure out what was going on in my head.

Please, please, please, stop.

Please, I need a break. I need time to understand what's been happening to me.

For a while the visions stopped and I started to get my head around them. At least, I thought I was.

I walked a lot, trying to figure out why I was having these experiences. Even though I'd had a bit of a break, my mind was still filled with everything that had happened; it was like a whirlpool in the middle of rapids, just like the tumultuous confusion they'd mentioned.

I wrote a lot but every time my head cleared and I thought, *I've got it*, the confusion returned and my mind went into a tailspin.

Spirit had said, *"From confusion comes clarity."*

So I supposed clarity would come although I was impatient.

I knew that the misinterpretation of the visions caused the confusion but I didn't want to acknowledge it. If I interpreted them correctly, my mind cleared and the fog lifted. If I interpreted them incorrectly, my mind spun and the fog descended.

For as long as I could remember, I had been seeing a pair of leather sandals with long straps that wrap around the ankles, hanging from a peg in the back of my mind. One day in Melbourne, I felt an intense desire to make them.

It took me a couple of days to get the materials together and find a pattern to match what I'd been seeing, which came from of my leatherwork books. I found an offcut of 5mm bull hide at a tannery for the under sole, plus two small brass buckles and two brass D-rings. I had a piece of 3mm embossing leather left over from some shoulder bags I had made for the upper sole. I also had a few belts I'd made so I cut up two for the straps. I found small brass nails at a nearby wholesaler to nail the upper and under soles together, which I also glued with a rubber solution.

There was a loop for the big toe and a bigger one for the other toes then the straps ran back, crossing over on the top of the foot, through a loop on each side and wrapping around the ankle and calf. Once they were finished, I put them on and went for a walk, wearing them to the local shops to see how they felt.

The first person I came across when I got there took one look at me and said, "I like your Jesus sandals."

And there I was thinking that it was over. That maybe there was going to be no more weird things happen to me. And then Jesus used a pair of sandals to say hello in a way that wouldn't freak me out.

I guessed that meant my break was over.

A couple of weeks later, I dreamt that I took a piece of leather and some waxed linen thread and attached my fifty millimetre clear quartz crystal ball to the top of the staff I got from Mum and Dad's farm. I had cut the leather so that when wrapped around the crystal ball, there was a circle on top and four teardrop shapes on the sides of the exposed quartz, one at each quarter. This piece of leather was wrapped around the crystal ball and the ends were bound to the staff with the waxed linen thread.

I woke up amused at the dream because it was something I wouldn't think of doing myself. So, just for fun, I did it.

An Archangel's Gift

I trimmed a little off the staff's length to align the crystal ball with my eye height while I was in bare feet, because that was how it was in the dream.

The four teardrop shapes symbolised fire, water, earth and air. The exposed circle on the top symbolised Spirit. The four teardrop shaped areas also represented the archangels: Mickhael as the representative of fire: Gabriel as the representative of water: Uriel as the representative of earth, and Raphael as the representative of air. The circle also symbolised conscious connection with the Divine.

The leather binding symbolised my passion for leatherwork. That told me that wherever this journey took me, I would be passionate about it.

The night after fixing the crystal ball to my staff, I had another dream about it. I dreamt that I inset four spirals of crystals and carved four names of ancient power in runes between them. I coloured the runes red with dragon's blood ink and the crystals I used in the dream were Garnet, Lapis lazuli, Emerald, and Citrine. One of those four names I carved was of the third spiritual entity from above the car accident, the one I call Farronell.

Again I did as the dream instructed. It took me three days, but I got it done. It looked pretty cool, like a wizard's staff.

Then again, I dreamt about the staff, though I had thought it was finished.

That dream showed me binding the staff for a further three hundred millimetres with a spiral of leather that was bound at each end with linen thread.

That was an easy one: it only took about an hour. Then it definitely looked finished.

I used the same leather for that binding as I had to bind the crystal ball; only this time I used a long strip about twenty millimetres wide.

I quite liked the upgraded version of my staff. If I had been a wizard, it would have suited me perfectly.

Then I dreamt that I carved the entire prophecy, which Jesus had given me in Canberra, in a spiral along the rest of the staff.

I just laughed and said, "It won't fit."

The following night, I had the same dream. In it, I carved the entire prophecy in runes and stained them red with dragon's blood ink. I didn't believe the dream. It told me that the prophecy will fit but I didn't think it would. I would have had to carve over twelve hundred runes on that little bit of wood. The part left to carve on was only 93cm long. It just didn't seem to be enough.

Night after night, I had the same dream. In the dream, I sat carving the prophecy into the wood with just a small craft knife and my bare hands, meticulously cutting and staining along a spiral path.

Night after night, I received the same guidance: the prophecy would fit on my staff.

An Archangel's Gift

I did not, I could not, bring myself to believe it. Logically, in my mind, the full prophecy would never fit on that small piece of wood.

Over and over in my mind, I said, *It won't fit. It won't fit.*

Thursday 7:00a.m.

I had the same dream for ten nights in a row and it was driving me nuts. It was growing more demanding and insistent.

It wouldn't fit; I knew it wouldn't, but seeing as how he wouldn't let go of this, I was going to prove to him that the prophecy *would not fit* on my staff.

Thursday 5:00p.m.

A very small, "Oops, it fits," trickled past my lips.

I had just spent the entire day very carefully making a fool of myself. I didn't know why I thought Jesus would ask me to do something that was impossible. I should have known, *he* would have known it would fit.

I had spent that day setting out the necessary spiral as shown to me in the dream and drew the prophecy onto the staff with a black waterproof marker pen. I marked all of the runes that make up the prophecy onto the staff, and they fit perfectly. I felt a little, or maybe a lot, embarrassed after all of my jumping up and down yelling, "It won't fit!"

I decided to start carving the runes the next day.

I didn't dream about carving the prophecy into the staff again once I began, which was a relief, but I had another dream.

I was making everything I needed to go on a solitary journey into previously unknown territory. In the dream, it was made clear that I could not make the journey until I personally had made everything I would need.

I didn't understand.

After the first day of carving and staining runes my fingers were sore and bruised from using a small craft knife on the hard wood. I thought it would probably take weeks to finish it.

Ten days later, and I was still carving runes. My fingers were bruised and bleeding with small cuts from the craft knife so I decided to have a couple of days off to let my fingers heal.

The dream of self-sufficiency meanwhile, came every night and every night since the first one. It was the same dream each time, and yet each night it was different. In the dream, I made everything I needed for the journey the dream thought I was going to take.

I still didn't understand and I hadn't dreamt about the staff since I started carving runes but I continued to work on carving the prophecy into the staff. I worked at it for a few days until my fingers were too sore to continue, then took a couple of days off while my fingers healed. It was painful but I couldn't have stopped if I'd wanted to, which I didn't.

I continued carving, driven to finish it.

I still had that same dream where I made everything I needed for a journey, every night while I carved the staff, and yet I could not, at that time, understand what it meant. The more I tried to understand it, the more questions I had.

I finally carved and stained the last rune. It had taken me nearly two months to carve and stain around fourteen hundred runes and I felt like the whole time I was waiting for my fingers to stop hurting so I could do more.

The staff really looked good and I was very proud of what I had achieved.

Here is the prophecy, given to me by Jesus, then carved into my staff: (Interpreted in Chapter 46.)

1:1 In the days that number nine,
1:2 from the New World will arise, the prophet Elijah,
1:3 to bring forth and unfurl the Faith of the One,
1:4 to express the word of Divinity,
1:5 at a time when darkness and light
1:6 fight for dominance in the world of man.

Edward Spellman

2:1 *The angels will walk once more*
2:2 *upon the world's surface,*
2:3 *and their children shall sing celebratory songs,*
2:4 *announcing the return of newness,*
2:5 *and the rebirth of Jerusalem.*

3:1 *The Goddess reign shall be complete,*
3:2 *with the Lords once more,*
3:3 *and rebirth, and beginnings beyond beginning,*
3:4 *will affect the world and the people of all lands.*

4:1 *Light will be seen for eternity throughout all lands*
4:2 *as darkness creeps amid despair*
4:3 *attempting to dissemble,*
4:4 *and wake the fears of many,*
4:5 *the fears of many are really the fears of one,*
4:6 *and the one, is self.*

5:1 *Dreams of heaven many must sell,*
5:2 *the crimes of one will bring about*
5:3 *the announcement of hell.*

6:1 *False prophets ride upon the winds of fear,*
6:2 *dragon's breath lights fear,*
6:3 *in the hearts of man and woman.*

An Archangel's Gift

7:1 Avarice is the core to understanding the old,
7:2 the old is the core to establishing the new.
7:3 As stars fall and worlds quake,
7:4 the brilliance of truth may come too late.

8:1 Fear of prophecy and truth lie still,
8:2 the heart of man,
8:3 a stone to be shattered at will.

9:1 In a land where the tall poppies grow,
9:2 and are ruthlessly cut asunder,
9:3 rise the stars of the Southern Cross,
9:4 to bring forth an end to plunder.

10:1 Of peace on Earth and goodwill to all,
10:2 some may know it,
10:3 but it will bring about the downfall of all.

11:1 All That Is may come again,
11:2 that which was holds no power.
11:3 Travel the roads that lead to the heart,
11:4 from the heart, the soul doth start,
11:5 from dreams and wishes, life becomes art.

12:1 Peace is the gift that cannot be held,
12:2 the sound of the bell, announces the fall, of hell.

After I finished the staff, I asked what it was for, and was told. *"To help you on your journey."*

As my journey was into self-awareness, that meant I had my staff and the prophecy carved into it to help me.

I had to ask myself, *But how? How were they going to do that?*

At about the same time I finished carving the staff I was given a message from Archangel Mickhael, *"Your mind will call up your past life as you progress in the balance of your training, slowly at first, with more rapidity later. There is a reason for this. You must be able to withstand the lure of former ties of family and nations, of friends and home. In your case, that is particularly vital, Edward."*

And I wondered, *am I supposed to stay in a state of tumultuous confusion?*

An Archangel's Gift

Chapter 18
Self Sufficiency

Each night while I was carving the prophecy, I had a repetitive dream. Unlike the insistent dreams of carving the staff, it was a continuation of the same dream of self-sufficiency. It felt like reading a book as each night I began from where I left off the night before. The full dream took two months.

During those dreams, I continued to make everything I needed for my solitary journey. I had to source materials, learn new skills, seek advice, design and make everything I would need which included clothing, a water bottle, belt, shoes, knife, backpack and a waterproof poncho, along with baking my own travel cakes.

The dream began the night after my first day of carving the prophecy and continued until it was finished. My solitary journey was somehow running parallel to, or in tandem with, the prophecy on the staff but I really didn't understand why.

I understood the self-sufficiency aspect, as I undertook this journey into self-awareness alone and no one could help, or take it for me.

The dreams also told me to become spiritually self-sufficient; to do it myself, to listen to my own internal guidance and trust it.

After two months of the same dream, I welcomed a change and completing the carving of the prophecy had triggered a new one.

I was standing on a forest path, surrounded by a dense mist—the mists of time. I wore the clothes and shoes I had made in the previous dream, and had everything else with me. In my right hand, I held the completed staff.

The mist swirled and billowed in a wind I couldn't feel and it was so thick, I couldn't see my feet. I took a step forward, tentatively feeling my way with my completed staff. I was learning to trust and put one foot down at a time upon my new path.

I took another step, then another and another. At each step, the mist thinned and soon I saw the path laid out before me, so I moved forward confidently.

It seemed to me as though it would be difficult to see what I was supposed to do next for a while, but eventually I would get where I was going, slowly and step by step.

I kept hearing Jesus say, *"Remember, Edward, everything is connected."*

Around this time, I was starting to think I was a bit weird. It seemed that most people didn't have experiences like these but at the same time, I didn't go around talking about it, or asking others if they had visions, so how was I to know? I watched people go about their daily lives and believed, from my observations, they were not seeing visions but I wasn't game enough to ask.

I had found a park with some beautiful old trees where, from time to time, I sat to meditate. One day I was meditating under a particularly gorgeous old tree and saw a vision of a clearing in a forest on the side of a mountain. And, as strange as it may seem, I was preparing to crucify myself.

From the side of the clearing where the crucifix was to be raised, there was a beautiful view down the length of a gorgeous river valley, with the fresh scent of a rainforest in the air.

I had three nails in my left hand. They were about six or seven inches long, the heads of the nails were circular and about one inch across, and all three nails were sharp enough to pierce the skin with no other force than their own weight; I had made the nails myself.

The cross lay on the ground at the side of the clearing furthest from the valley and a fresh hole had been dug to stand it in.

I walked over and lay myself down on the cross. On my wrists and feet I had marked the positions for the nails. I passed a nail to someone; that someone was also me.

With a little help from myself, I nailed myself to the cross and stood it up. I hung up there for a while as my friends were having a picnic toward the edge of the clearing.

As the day came to an end, I was suddenly not crucified anymore and there was no sign that I had been.

The vision told me that I had been crucifying myself because Jesus and Uriel suggested I write a book, but luckily, I would eventually get on with it. I was also learning to surrender to the Divine and follow my guidance.

Not long after that vision, I was on my way home from Chadstone Shopping Centre when an intensely emotional vision hit me hard. I nearly crashed the car.

Although driving, I also found myself sitting cross-legged on the rich, moist soil of a forest floor. Huge eucalypts towered above and tree ferns surrounded me. Everything around me was in deep shadow.

As I sat, tears welled in my eyes and streamed down my cheeks, making it hard to drive. Deep emotional sobs racked my throat. I could feel the sickness, or dis-ease in Mother Earth, and I felt love, compassion and empathy from her.

The tears rolled down my cheeks as I leant forward and placed my hands, palms down and with my fingers stretched out, onto the rich shadowed soil in front of me. As my hands touched the earth, I sensed movement from beneath them; like ripples spreading in a pond after a pebble had been thrown in. Light came, washing away the shadow and healing Mother Earth. Soon the forest was enveloped in golden light and everything was healthy again.

The experience left me with an intense sense of satisfaction and joy, and of course, a wet face.

I had been walking a lot trying to work out the stiffness in my body from too many years laying bricks and busting myself up in that car accident, as well as trying to work out what was happening to me. I began to see, every time I closed my eyes, Hebrew letters written in fire. They flashed at the top right quadrant of my vision. It didn't matter how long I closed my eyes, they were there and continued at the same rate; two or three characters per second.

The Hebrew fire writing had been going on again all day. At night as I tried to go to sleep it continued unabated, keeping me awake for hours and kept going for about two and a half days.

It stopped for two weeks and then they came back for another couple of days.

I had no idea what it all meant.

I was going crazy trying to understand the Hebrew letters of fire. I knew that they were the, *Word of God*, but why had I been seeing them? What did *he* want with me? Why wouldn't *he* just leave me alone?

For five months I had the phone numbers. I picked up the phone and started to dial, then put the phone down. Sometimes I even finished dialing but put the phone down before anyone could answer. I must have attempted to call at least a hundred times.

Then one day, I scraped up the necessary courage.

With my curiosity in full swing, I rang both the Catholic bishop of Melbourne and the most prominent rabbi I could find in the phone book to see if I could get any help as to why I was seeing Hebrew letters of fire and what they meant.

I didn't get past either of their secretaries, who both got angry and accused me of perpetrating a hoax.

I never did find out what they were scared of but I assumed they were scared because of their anger.

Time passed and I asked a few priests about the Hebrew letters of fire but they had no answers for me either.

More time passed and whenever I got the opportunity, I would ask my questions. "Why did I see Hebrew letters of fire? What do they mean?"

No one had any answers.

And again more time passed and I woke in the dark of night and wrote angrily in my diary by torchlight. I was frustrated with not knowing so I wrote, *Why the fire writing? Hebrew letters, written in fire are the Word of God; that I understand. But what I don't understand is what they say and why you are presenting them to me.*

As soon as I finished writing down my frustrations, this answer came:

"Rather than thinking about what the Hebrew letters of fire mean as the written word, think about what they mean symbolically. They are my trademark of sorts, and I mean: I am God, and I am here always. I have access to you at all times, and also that I can speak to you in a language that you think you do not understand. Case in point, symbolism. They mean I am immanent and interested in your life, Edward, my son. They also deliver information that you require on your journey and this will filter through at the appropriate times. The Hebrew letters of fire have many meanings for you and as you delve into them, they will come to you."

Having received my answer I wrote, "It's nice to finally receive some answers and understand. That's so cool. Thank you."

I went to sleep with a smile on my face.

An Archangel's Gift

Chapter 19
My Suit of Golden Armour

I was missing the family farm so I put myself through a guided meditation and used my imagination to go for a walk through the familiar bush there.

Maybe down by the river, I thought, *and along the old water-race cut into the side of the hill from the gold mining days.*

I got comfortable, took a deep centering breath and drifted…

I walked along the river flat just past the old broken down tractor, already there when Mum and Dad bought the farm. The track ran along the bottom of the hill, snaking its way between eucalypts and tea tree scrub. At the end of the flat, I came to a fence and passed it, heading off the track and into the trees. There, a trench marked the lower end of the water-race and I followed it. The trench ended and the rest of the race was cut into the side of the hill following the river.

An Archangel's Gift

I walked along, using memory as a guide, listening to the river bubbling below me and the wind in the trees. As I walked along, the scenery slipped from what I knew, as though someone else took over my meditation with his own script. It was Jesus, I suspected.

While I had intended to follow the path of the water-race to the big pool and sit on a ledge and dangle my feet a ways above the water, a waterfall suddenly appeared in front of me. It ran over a big slab of rock that had a gap behind it.

I moved closer and saw a cave behind the waterfall. It wasn't very big but it was large enough for me to stand upright so I entered.

The walls were dark, healthy earth with tree roots here and there. I walked deeper into the cave and crystals poked from the earth: amethyst, citrine, quartz, garnet, emerald, and many more which felt warm and welcoming.

Deeper and deeper I walked, until as I got to a point where there was almost no light from the entrance; I saw light up ahead and continued. Soon I came to the other end and stepped out onto a sunlit, grass covered shelf high up on the side of a mountain. The hills of the farm were a world away from there.

The shelf was only about an acre in size and nearby, Pegasus was grazing. In the distance, I saw the purple haze of mountains with what looked like large birds cruising high above the clouds. Far below me stretched verdant forests and grasslands with a scattering of lakes and rivers.

As I realised that I couldn't get off the shelf, Pegasus approached and spoke to my mind without words and invited me for a ride. I swung myself up onto his broad back and held tight as he leapt into the air. He was pure white with no blemishes on either his body or wings and smelt more like flowers than a bird or a horse.

We flew from the mountainside toward a small lake. As we came closer to the lake, I saw an island at its center.

Pegasus landed on the shore across from the island and I slipped to the earth, giving him a gentle pat of thanks. I intended to swim the rest of the way. I needed to go to the island and I had to get there by myself.

As I stepped into the lake, I did not experience the normal sensations of walking into water. The temperature was the same as my body and there was almost no sensation of being in water at all. I dived forward and swam; and while I swam I looked around me. The visibility was perfect; it was as clear as the air above. The lake bottom was covered in small pebbles and there were no fish or plants, yet as I swam I knew I was moving through the *waters of life*. It felt real and yet symbolic at the same time.

Soon I came to the island and walked out of the water, my clothes dried instantly, giving this place a magickal air. I headed toward the centre of this small island.

An Archangel's Gift

Soon I came to an area paved with polished stone, as though it was the floor of some long gone ancient building. The area was about thirty or forty paces across and at the other end was a set of seven steps. At the top were two stone columns and between the columns, sat the High Priestess of the tarot. She looked just as she did in Pamela Colman Smith's painting for the Ryder-Waite Tarot card.

As I approached the steps, I said to her, "It's okay. I know you're real."

As soon as I had spoken those words, the priestess transformed, stepping forward she morphed into the female aspect of Divinity—the Goddess.

She approached as the divine feminine in physical form. Her ankle length white gown seemed to be alive as it moved and wove around her voluptuous body. First showing one curve then another, her hips swaying as she walked toward me.

The Goddess whispered something to me that I couldn't hear on a conscious level. She bent and gently kissed me on the forehead, and then she stepped back a little and said, *"I have a gift for you."*

She presented me with a full suit of golden armour and said, *"Take this. It will protect you."*

I looked down at the golden armour and when I looked up again, she was gone. Then I saw a vision within the vision of myself out in space wearing the armour and sitting on an old wooden fruit crate looking down at planet Earth. Then I was back in my lounge room, opening my eyes to a rainy afternoon.

I considered its meaning. Realisation dawned that by presenting the High Priestess, the vision was telling me that I was experiencing a time of influence from higher sources. Spirit was guiding me to be alert to divine guidance and inspiration as I moved along my path.

When I thought of the tunnel, it led to another world where colours were brighter, the air was clearer and mystical creatures were alive. That indicated I was headed in a direction very different to where I had come from.

The crystals in the cave spoke of prosperity along my path; perhaps representing life's riches awaiting me as I continued to uncover the mysteries of Spirit.

I didn't understand being submerged in the *waters of life* but I knew that the armour was for my protection, without knowing what I needed to be protected from.

I was starting to feel silly saying, *I saw a vision; I saw a vision,* but there were no other words for them. Even the dreams that told me how to make my staff weren't dreams: they were instructional visions. They were intense and profound in indescribable ways. They were life changing.

I began to lose myself, *or perhaps to find myself,* in this world of visions, dreams, and prophecy. My fears were abating as my curiosity increased and I began to lose touch with what happened between visions as they swirled in my mind.

In another vision, I saw a small lake with a water wheel attached to a workshop on the far shore. The water wheel was not functioning as it should have because the wooden water-race that normally would have carried water from a nearby dam had lots of leaks in it and no water reached the wheel to power it.

As I watched, the vision showed me the stationary water wheel, then the leaky water-race, then the dam full of water. It repeated this series several times.

I was shown inside the workshop, then the wheel, the race and dam again, then returned to the workshop.

Okay I get it, I thought as the vision unfolded. *The workshop won't operate without the water wheel and the water wheel won't function without water from the dam.*

I asked, "Will working on my book repair the water-race?"

Suddenly, water flowed along the race but not enough to get the wheel functioning.

The vision repeated its sequence several more times before I asked, "Will delving into my visions and myself and writing about it repair the water-race?"

The race filled with water. The water flowed down to the water wheel and it began functioning as it should. It began to turn. The workshop and water wheel were both reflections of me, so to function as I should, I needed to delve into my visions and write about them. Turning them over and flowing with them

Then the vision switched between the water wheel and the dam. First it showed the wheel, then *up* to the dam; then the wheel, the dam; the wheel, the dam. The vision was pointing out that the dam was *above* the water wheel.

"What is above?"

Spirit's above. Divinity is above.

And with that the vision calmed, the water wheel began to turn, and a sense of completion like I had just turned the last page of a good book flowed through me. I took that to mean I had gotten it right.

As the water wheel began to turn, I heard. *"The goal is not to finish the book, although the book being finished will be a reflection of your reconnection with the Divine."*

"We have to allow darkness equal access to you—you have to be the one to choose and every thought, word, and deed is involved in those choices. They try to steer you away; we nudge you back."

"Have you been white lighting? Who do you think encourages you not too?"

I came to understand that white lighting was a way to use my imagination to cleanse myself of, and protect myself from, negative and disharmonious energies. One method was to imagine a white light waterfall flowing over me and washing away the unwanted energies. Another was to form a point of white light at my centre and imagine it expanding and pushing the negative and disharmonious energies out of my body and energy field.

I found that practicing this regularly generated a level of protection.

Chapter 20
The Emerald Cave

Jayson had also moved to Melbourne and was again sitting in a chair preparing himself. He softened his grip on consciousness and closed his eyes.

Archangel Mickhael energetically slipped into Jayson's energy system and began to speak to us. I received yet another message from Jesus through Mickhael's mouthpiece, *"Stop hiding your light under a bushel."*

I didn't know what he was talking about and felt frustrated and confused again like he was shouting advice I didn't understand from the sideline.

During that last channel, I received another message from Jesus, again through Archangel Mickhael. *"Someday, my son, you will understand why it is that I stand back and let you do this alone."*

Sometimes *someday* seemed to be a very long way away and sometimes, I wanted to throw this book as far away as I could, while at the same time, holding on to it as hard as I could.

Not long after Jayson's channeling, I woke up one morning with a strong desire to go meditate by the ocean so I headed off to find a nice spot. I looked at the map and found a spot that looked good. There was a lighthouse out past Geelong at the entrance to Port Phillip Bay and I headed there.

Once there, I walked down toward the ocean and found myself an alcove worn into the sandstone by wind and wave. I sat, listening to the waves lapping against the stone shelf below me. I closed my eyes and drifted to the sound of the sea; then called for protection and drifted into meditation.

A landscape of barren hills, mountains and valleys, all devoid of life filled my vision. It was opaque green, as though made of weathered Emerald.

As I moved deeper into the landscape, there was a canyon that I followed to a cavern. As I entered, I saw that the walls, floor and roof were all smooth and rounded as though from a continuous flow of water, although there was none there now. I stood in the tunnel of an underground river that ran through an emerald mountain. The floor sloped slightly downward and there were no shadows; somehow, the cavern was well lit.

Further into the cavern, I found a pristine and clear pool of water that stretched from wall to wall.

From where I stood, there was a drop of about ten feet to the surface of the pool. On the side of the pool furthest from me, the water came almost up to a wide stone shelf. On the other side, there was a rough track that could get me around the pool.

I noticed men dressed in black sneaking toward the pool, looking furtively about without seeing me. They came to the edge and looked into the pool. There were riches beyond their wildest dreams there at the bottom. They took the path to the lower side and prepared to go after the treasure.

As they moved into the pool, they discovered it was much deeper than it looked due to its clarity. They dove for their treasure and filled bag after bag, which they put on the far shelf. When they finally ran out of bags to carry treasure, they prepared to leave. Before they could do so, however, what they had seen as a path, morphed into the guardian of the treasure. There stood a magnificent emerald green dragon.

The dragon spoke. *'Take what you will from this place. What you can leave with is yours. I will not stop you, yet, I cannot help you as you have used my back to get to the treasure and I am bound to help only once."*

Having spoken, the dragon turned from them and went back along the path I had followed to get there.

An Archangel's Gift

With the dragon gone, the men proceeded to collect what they came for. They picked up their treasure and looked for a way out. They soon found that the only way out of the cavern was across the pool and the only way across the pool was along the dragon's back. But the dragon had left.

Try as they might, they could not make their way past the pool. The wall on my side was smooth, without any hand or footholds, and there was no way out from the other side either. They swam across to this side of the pool carrying their treasure and tried to climb out. Refusing to let go of their newly acquired riches, they spluttered and splashed, cursed and kicked, until the weight of their treasure dragged them to the bottom and the cavern was quiet again.

The guardian returned and took his place along the side of the pool, blending into the emerald of the cavern walls.

I moved to the edge, dove in and swam to the other side where, as I climbed out onto the lower shelf, the dragon turned to greet me. *"Take what you will from this place. What you can leave with is yours. I will not stop you and I am bound to help. One favor I can grant, and only one."*

I bowed to the guardian in respect. "Thank you."

I dove into the pool again, and down to the treasure. Amongst a pile of gold and gems, I saw the hilt of a sword. As I pulled it free, I exposed the edge of what looked like a silver platter with a heavy gold rim and retrieved it from the pile.

I swam to the surface with what I had found and climbed out of the pool, sat down on the edge, and took my time to inspect prizes. I had a three-foot sword with a highly polished double-edged steel blade that tapered from about an inch and a half at the hilt, to a point. The cross guard and pommel were gold and decorated with endless knot work while the handgrip was silver wire. Putting the sword down I took up my second prize and what I thought at first was a platter, was actually a shield of exquisite beauty and workmanship. It was made of polished silver and about two feet wide with a rim of gold about as thick as my index finger and also decorated with endless knot work. Covering three quarters of the face of the shield was a matching five-pointed star with a single point facing upward and with the same decoration as the rim. The orientation of the star means that it symbolised the sacred feminine.

I was a bit stunned and didn't really know what to make of them. Despite being submerged, the sword and shield were in perfect condition.

The dragon's voice rumbled in the cavern, *"Ask your favor."*

"Carry me from this place and set me down safely where there is green grass beneath my feet," I said.

An Archangel's Gift

A short time later, I stood on a green hilltop and watched the dragon's flight. In my right hand, I held the sword and on my left arm was the shield.

Waves crashed on the beach. I took a deep breath and opened my eyes to the sunlight playing amongst the waves.

A seal basked in the sun about twenty feet away. He must have turned up while I was meditating.

Now I had the shield and sword to go with my suit of golden armour. And they looked like they were part of the same set.

When I looked at the vision and asked what it meant, I heard. *"There are treasures within the depths of your mind that you have access to that others do not."*

After looking at them for a while their meaning became obvious. The sword symbolised the male aspect of divinity, or God and the shield symbolised the female and Goddess. Together, as a matching set, they represented God and Goddess in balance. The same applied to the gold and silver in both the sword and the shield. The gold is the God and sacred masculine—the silver is the Goddess and the sacred feminine.

That there was no scabbard for the sword meant that it was always ready to act in my defense.

Edward Spellman

Then I looked up emerald and found that it was the sacred stone of the Goddess; and the stone of hope and prophecy.

An Archangel's Gift

Chapter 21
Horses

I was working at a nursing home where the other staff members on my shift were a bit grouchy and negative in the mornings. They even took offence when I came to work in a light-hearted mood and actually attacked me for it. It was as though they were afraid of feeling good.

I told them that every day the sun came up was a good day, and the sun came up every day.

They told me that there was something wrong with a person who came to work in a good mood all the time so it had to be false.

After a couple of months, I woke one morning with a question repeating over and over again in the depths of my mind. *"Does your heart sing as you rise with the dawn and the wonders of nature unfold?"*

"Yes, my heart does sing as I rise with the dawn and the wonders of nature unfold."

An Archangel's Gift

That sounded good so, I wrote it down and immediately another filled its space. I wrote that one down too, and then another came. Soon I had a poem of these questions:

Does your heart sing
as you rise with the dawn
and the wonders of nature unfold?

Does your heart swell
and your soul sing with joy
as a child sleeps in your arms?

Does your heart sing
when you sit on the grass
or gaze from a mountain's top?

Does your heart brim with love
at the sounds you can hear
as you sit by a brook in the forest?

Does your heart sing
as the sun tickles your skin
or the moon shines softly at night?

Does your heart skip a beat
and your eyes shine bright

as your lover walks through the door?

*Does your heart sing
as waves crash at your feet
and a wind plays with the trees in a forest?*

*Does your heart glow
as you come to know
that we are all part of the One?
Does your heart sing?*

It felt good just to reread it.

Whenever there were grumpy or negative people about, I heard those words spoken in the depths of my mind. It was as though someone were quietly whispering it to a child just before sleep.

Then I heard in a soft whisper, *"Don't be afraid. I'm always here."*

I guessed that meant that I was the child…a spiritual child. I didn't mind that, it brought a smile to my face and a glow to my belly.

Around that time another vision kept recurring. I guess I wasn't paying enough attention to it, or perhaps I was having trouble working it out. And maybe I just wasn't ready to understand it for a while.

An Archangel's Gift

The vision came again so I sat at my computer to write. I put my fingers on the keyboard and nothing.

Okay! So, what am I missing? This is different in some way, but how? The visions usually seemed to want to be recorded.

Ah! I got it.

This was definitely not a dream as every time it happened, I was wide awake. Nor was it like the other visions I had. What was different was the way it was experienced. It felt somehow like a shape-shifting experience. I'd had others like that and brushed them aside but this one didn't seem to want to be brushed aside and that in itself stated its relevance, so here it is.

My unshod hooves kicked up a little dust as I moved along with the herd. I saw my reflection in the eye of a nearby horse, my two-tone colouring, reddish brown with large patches of white, told me that I existed in both the physical and spiritual worlds simultaneously. My reflection in the other horse's eye told me that this experience was a reflection of my life. I drifted along on the outskirts of the herd, hardly noticed by the other horses.

Moving off to the side to avoid the dust, I saw something off to the left. *What is that?* I wandered over to take a look.

Nothing there. Just a minute, there it is again.

I went for a look, and again there was nothing there.

That pattern continued for some time until suddenly I realised I had wandered away from the herd.

Perhaps I should go back. No, there it is again. What is that?

Again and again I tried to catch up with the elusive shadow until I was at a point high on the ridge bordering the grazing lands. From down there it appeared that those ridges and hills were impassable but I had just come through them unaware of what I was doing.

As I looked in the direction away from the herd, I saw I had come to a higher plain where many horses were grazing, although there, it was different. Down below, I saw the herd pushing and shoving, competing for the best grass and the cleanest water; the horses were always jostling each other.

Here however, the horses were all spread out. No one was shoving anyone else. There was plenty for all.

On the other hand, when the herd moved, it destroyed everything in its path. The horses up the front got the best grass and the cleanest water leaving the majority to fight over what was left.

The high plain was lush and green and abundant where the grazing lands below were only like this before the herd got to it. Having been guided to that place, I just wanted to run back to the herd and share with everyone what I had found.

An Archangel's Gift

As I looked over that prosperous land, I understood that the shadow I had been chasing was my guidance, Jesus; and that by following, although I may not have understood where he was leading me, it would be equal to those prosperous grazing lands of the high plain. I also understood that his guidance was, for now, focused on writing. Writing the book would lead me to a place of deeper awareness, a place much more prosperous than where I was.

Chapter 22

Snowballs

I was just minding my own business, pottering around the house when a garden appeared before me. There, many different types of fruit and vegetables grew but they were stunted, undernourished and ill formed because weeds stifled them.

I saw workers enter the garden. They removed all the weeds and then fertilised and watered the plants. Weeks and months became seconds as all the plants grew, bloomed and bore fruit before my eyes. Although the garden was old, it had never been as abundant or healthy as it was then.

I understood.

That was me after Jesus came into my life and reinvigorated and cleansed my spiritual belief system, which incorporated my perceptions of reality and self-awareness.

I was the garden and the weeds were the negative aspects of myself, which corrupted the positive aspects, fruits and vegetables. Apparently, I needed a good weeding, watering and fertilising. It sounded like interesting times ahead.

I had a sense that Jesus was playing with me and that at some point I would forget to be afraid of the game and start enjoying it. With that thought in mind, I experienced another vision. I saw, tasted, felt, smelt and found myself in the middle of this experience.

I was sitting on the top of a snow-covered mountain with Jesus sitting beside me and we dangled our feet over the edge of a shelf at the top of a long, steep slope.

He reached into the snow, took a handful and formed it into a snowball. He showed it to me and said, *"You are this snowball, my son. Watch."*

He put the snowball down and gave it a gentle push and it was off, racing down the mountain. The snowball dodged rocks and trees. It bumped into, or was bumped by other snowballs. Finally it reached the end of its journey down the mountain.

I was filled with a new sense of awareness as I sat with him at the top of the mountain; safe with Jesus ever by my side. I looked about, amazed that my awareness could expand so much. "Jesus," I asked, "is this it, or is there more?"

By way of reply, he gave me a gentle nudge and that was all it took to start me moving forward. I was off as a snowball, racing down the mountain, dodging rocks and trees, occasionally bumping into, or being bumped into by other snowballs, during my trip down the mountainside.

Finally I reached the bottom and rolled to a stop. I looked about myself and realised with amazement that with my trip down the mountain, my awareness had again expanded. I felt complete; I felt that I had become all that I could possibly become.

I was aglow with wisdom and knowledge. I was aware of things that not long before I would not have believed. *So, this is the path to enlightenment?*

I felt my awareness expand, become deeper and more profound. Then I was back at the top of the mountain. I sensed Jesus beside me and acknowledged him without words.

Then I felt a chill and a thought slipped into my mind, *What's that over to the left?*

I leant over to take a look.

In leaning, I set myself in motion again and off I went rolling down the mountain. On my way down, I dodged trees and rocks, bumped into or was bumped into by other snowballs until eventually I came to rest at the bottom.

That happened again and again. Yet every time, no matter what occurred on the way down the mountain, when I reached the bottom, my awareness, my wisdom and knowledge had grown more deeply.

After countless trips down the mountain of life, I found myself again at the mountaintop with Jesus beside me. We sat there making snowballs and gently setting them off on their journeys. I enjoyed watching the progression of the souls I helped along their paths. I smiled as I saw them trying to dodge a lesson that needed to be learnt, only to see them land smack into it on the next round. I laughed when they got to the bottom of the slope thinking they had made it, that they had it all figured out, and yet I knew, always, there was more to learn.

I sat on the mountain beside Jesus, my entire being aglow with love and joy. Jesus was with me; I felt his love, his wisdom, his joy and his amusement.

I asked him to share his source of amusement and he did. With a gentle shove and lots of encouragement, he laughed and slapped me on the shoulder; I was off down the mountain of life once again although, as I rolled down the mountain, I realised I was not out of control. I could miss obstacles. I could even choose to jump some of them, nudge other snowballs to safety and shepherd them through dangerous places in their lives. I could help others reach the bottom of the mountain. I learnt to use my skills and attributes, my awareness, knowledge and wisdom to help others to find their true paths as they tumbled down the mountain. He was showing me that each time a soul travelled down the path of life, it gathered wisdom and knowledge through its experience in the world. Then, in its following life, that accumulated wisdom and knowledge would express itself through the soul's interactions and experiences.

By that time, I settled into accepting visions as part of my life. Further, I think they were becoming my life.

The vision of the snowballs blew me away and I didn't stop smiling for days. Every time I thought about it, I burst out laughing at myself sitting on the top of the mountain with Jesus and thinking I had learnt it all. That was hilarious.

For a long time, I had thought that this book was it; that it was all I had to do, but not after that vision.

One day, I was thinking about this never-ending journey and wondering how other people dealt with the sort of stuff that had been happening to me. Out in my garden, just sitting and enjoying the feel of it around me, I felt the garden's embrace, that my garden liked me. As I sat there listening to the leaves in the light breeze, another vision began and I saw a dark grey cliff stretching as far as the eye could see to the left and to the right. The bottom of the cliff was out of sight but I could see the top.

Running horizontally across the cliff was a wide, easy path, crowded with people walking from left to right.

An Archangel's Gift

Everything was in shades of grey, like an old black and white photo or a silent movie.

The people had blank, grey faces, as though they had stockings pulled over them. They had no eyes, no mouths and no ears. Everybody moved blindly, deafly, dumbly forward as though none of them could use their senses.

From time to time, a traveller came across a small path that reminded me of a goat track as it wound its way up the cliff to the top. Some who found this path ignored it and moved along with the crowd, while others began to climb. As they climbed, they climbed out of shadow and into colour. As they climbed, their facial features filled in. As they climbed, they gained their sight.

Once these travellers reached the top, they found a world of light and colour. The air tasted cleaner. The food was more nourishing. The people on that higher plane were living in harmony with nature. This higher plane was a more spiritual place where those on a journey into self-awareness would eventually come to reside.

Lower down on the path along the cliff, those who ignored or were afraid to seek the higher plane continued along their seemingly easy path, only to disappear into shadow.

After thinking about it for a while, the vision showed me that there were things about to happen in the world that a percentage of people would not acknowledge and, in refusing to acknowledge those new energies, they rejected the opportunity to grow spiritually and therefore move onto a higher plane of awareness.

An Archangel's Gift

Chapter 23
That Day

Sometimes I found it difficult to write about the things I saw. I thought it was just a fear of what others may think, which I knew was silly.

Sometimes the only way I could write was to tell myself that no one else would read it anyway, while at the same time knowing that wasn't true.

When I asked Jesus why I was writing this book, he said, *"What's the point of having a story if you don't share it?"*

That didn't really make me feel any more comfortable. Sometimes it felt like he was asking me to bare my soul to the world and myself. With me being rather shy and introverted, that was a very big thing. I expected that writing down my experiences would help to change that, or at least make them easier to accept.

When I was little, my family would go to the local swimming pool on the weekends in summer. Mum and

Dad took my sister, five brothers and me. The swimming pool that we used to go to turned up as the venue for a vision.

In this vision, which was similar to one I saw earlier, I saw the pool as it was when I was a child but this time it had lots of coloured balls, about basketball size, floating in it.

Around the edge of the pool and in it, were lots of people trying to push and keep the balls beneath the surface. Some balls had only one person trying to keep them under, while others had several.

As I watched the scene, a ball occasionally broke free and burst from the water, fell back to the surface and floated there.

I noticed that the force used by the people to hold the balls under the water was the same force that caused the balls to break free and leap to the surface.

I understood that the balls were universal spiritual truths and those striving to submerge them were representations of my ego. Each time a ball, or truth, broke free and rose to the surface, it caused the hold on all of the others to weaken.

The truths were held down by my fears: fear of the unknown, fear of losing control. The fears were false in regards to my self, as the release and bringing truth to light would generate my freedom.

The extent of my reaction to the resurgent universal spiritual truth was in direct proportion to the depth that particular truth had been suppressed within me. My reaction could be expressed in either a relatively short-lived emotional break-through or, depending on my personality, a much longer and seemingly more sedate emotional break-through.

Just to make it interesting, once a truth chose to surface, there was nothing I could do to prevent it. Trying to supress it only caused emotional distress and tumultuous confusion, which I tended to create from time to time anyway.

I liked the idea that the resistance to something generated the energy that allowed it to break free. Repress something and in doing so, I forced it out.

While writing, I kept having experiences that I found difficult to describe. The result was that some of them appeared pretty bland. The ones that sound bland were the ones that were the most amazing or mind-boggling visions. The next vision was one of those.

Slowly I opened my eyes and looked about. I couldn't tell if I was awake or asleep.

Is this a dream or is it a vision? What's going on?

It was very strange. I couldn't see anything but a thick, white mist. I couldn't hear anything; couldn't feel anything. It wasn't hot and wasn't cold; temperature didn't exist in that place.

I asked myself, *Am I alive? Am I dead?*

There was no answer.

As I peered into the mist, it began to move and swirl. Half-seen shadows and hints of form teased my sight. The mist thinned and melted away and the forms and hints became people.

A crowd grew until there were perhaps several hundred people, from all walks of life and from many different cultures. The mist cleared and we were standing in the centre of a beautiful grassed valley.

If I had ever stood at the top of the world, I suspect it would have felt a bit like this. There was grass beneath our feet and a perfect blue cloudless sky above and the horizon looked a little strange in its precision. There was no fading of colour or hue, just the grassy hills and perfection of the sky.

As I looked around this delightful valley, it seemed as though I should know it. The folds of the land had the familiarity of a long-time lover. It felt like I knew all the intricacies of the landscape intimately but I couldn't quite place it.

Intuitively I knew everyone felt the same; they knew this place, yet none of them could say they'd been here before. The entire valley was covered with ankle length grass and scattered wildflowers.

To find a better vantage point, a small group of us headed for higher ground. After walking for what felt like several hours, although my watch had stopped so I couldn't be sure, we reached our goal, a high point overlooking the valley.

We turned to survey the place, for none of us quite believed this could be the physical world of our waking lives, and none believed our lives had ended. We stood agape at what lay before us. A chill ran down my spine as awareness of where we were slowly sank in.

Standing there overlooking the valley, we all had our right hands held in front of us at about waist height, fingers together, thumb tucked into the side, and the hand held slightly cupped. First, we looked down at our hands, then up and across the valley, then back down at our hands again. We looked into each other's eyes. No words were necessary. There was no doubt in our minds as to where we were and what day this was.

With a twinkle in my eye and a smile on my lips, I walked back with my companions to those gathered below. Quietly, we awaited that which we knew was coming.

In the centre of the valley, there were some strange reactions taking place. There were people walking about trying to call someone or other on their mobile phones while mumbling, "It's not time. It can't be time. I'm not ready. I need more time."

The phones didn't work and everyone's watches had stopped.

There were those who thought it was all an illusion or a dream, and that they would wake up soon. Or at least they hoped it was, and that they would.

I looked closely at the people with me in that place that exists outside of our perceptions of time and space; a place between time. Some people were frothing at the mouth and tearing at their hair. Others babbled incoherently, and yet, amongst all that confusion, the most noticeable were those with a knowing smile on their faces. There was an air of calm about them, of knowing and acceptance. Their influence radiated into the crowd, spreading calm.

Soon, an expectant hush encompassed us all.

The valley itself looked small at times, and at others it somehow gave off a feeling of immeasurable space. The people at the centre took up about as much space as would a pinch of salt in the palm of my hand.

Everything there seemed perfect: the grass, the shape of the landscape, the horizon, even the colour of the sky: a blue that went on forever. Even the light was perfect; I could see everything clearly in the valley, and it felt as though spring sunshine caressed my body.

I looked about the valley, at the people grouped in the centre, at the skyline. Then my gaze took in the grass, and the people beside me. I looked at the sky from horizon to horizon and back again.

Something was nagging at the back of my mind. I stared at the ground. I allowed my eyes to roam and then with a start, I looked back at that unblemished sky and stared into it. There were no clouds, no stars, no moon and no sun. But that shouldn't have surprised me as I looked again at my cupped right hand and then about the valley.

I laughed at myself for being surprised at there being no sun to cast a shadow when the light was pure, clear and perfect. Why should there be a sun? What use would a sun be as we stood there in the palm of the right hand of God on Judgement Day?

In front of us, the light shimmered and twisted. Space appeared to turn itself inside out and a judge's bench appeared before us. It was made of polished mahogany, had a gold embossed green leather top and there was a walnut gavel lying on it.

It looked strange because the top of the bench was solid and sat at about shoulder height, while the legs were vapour. The bench sat there looking both solid yet not, at the same time.

Again the light shimmered and appeared to turn itself inside out as a figure appeared behind the bench and took hold of the gavel. While everything else in the valley was easy to look at, I had to squint as I tried to focus on the figure behind the bench.

At first he or she appeared to be an old man with a white beard, then the maiden, the mother, the crone, then Zeus; or was it Isis? Then Odin, then another and another.

Everyone looked at the figure seated at the bench and we each saw something different.

The light shimmered then slowly settled and the figure came into focus. We all saw looking back at us that which we perceived as Divinity. The gods of our ancestors looked out over the crowd, and yet, within that twisting shimmering light, we all saw an aspect of ourselves returning our gaze.

The gavel fell and a voice whispered and boomed through the depths of my mind and yet the communication that followed was not verbal; it was so much more.

In its simplest form, it was that we are not judged by God or any other. We were told we were judged by ourselves through our every thought, word, and deed. And through our every thought, word, and deed, we drew to us both the appropriate reward and the appropriate punishment. Our thoughts, words and deeds attracted a response from the universe equal to their value. In essence, we got what we gave.

Therefore, if our thoughts, words and deeds were of a positive nature, the rewards that we reaped were also of a positive nature; while if they were of a negative nature, the rewards for those were of a negative nature.

There was so much depth to the message that it was difficult even to skim the surface. Also the communication made me aware that not only does this place exist outside of time and space, it always has and always will be. It exists in the time between the time that is now, in which we judge ourselves continuously from the day we are born until the day we die.

A miraculous part of this is that we, and no other, had the right and capability to forgive ourselves.

An Archangel's Gift

Chapter 24
Barren Ground

Despite my commitment to this journey, it was the scariest thing I'd ever been asked to do. I continued to reflect, pray and ask. *Why is this happening to me? Why do I have these visions?*

Jesus answered, *"Because you are in the right place."*

I would have liked to know what the hell that meant. Sometimes his cryptic answers drove me nuts, so I asked him about it and he told me, *"If I were to just give it to you, it would have no value. You do love a puzzle, so I give you what you need in a way that keeps you interested."*

I love Jesus with all my heart and soul and he knew exactly what to say to me to help me get through my moments of doubt and confusion. He also knew exactly how to encourage me to keep going despite my fears. And then at other times I wanted to slap him upside the head with a very large fish.

An Archangel's Gift

I'd been loitering around the house for a couple of days contemplating the visions and writing them down as I wondered, *what am I doing?*

I kept hearing, as I had been hearing for quite some time, just one word like it was whispered at the back of a cave and the echo bounced around without diminishing.

Pathfinder, pathfinder, pathfinder.
Pathfinder, pathfinder, pathfinder.

I sat down and meditated on the word, asking what path I would be finding.

Suddenly I understood. The path I was finding was my own, and this book, which was an articulation of my journey into self-awareness, would show me my path.

As I woke in the early morning hours, I saw before me a landscape of broken black stone through which there were two paths. One path, clear, broad and straight, went to the right. The other, more like a goat trail, was narrow and twisted in and around the rocky landscape to the left.

I moved along the right hand path until I came to a huge silver bowl filled with fruit. The bowl was about ten feet across and its rim sat lower than the path and there was a gap of about eighteen inches between the bowl and the depression it sat in that mirrored its shape.

As I stood before the bowl of almost perfect, ripe fruit piled before me, I saw just one little spot that could be straightened up. I leant over to move that one piece of fruit, and slipped through the ripe fruit on top into the bowl of stinking, rotten slop beneath the surface. I disappeared, swallowed whole by a bowl of rotten fruit.

Then I was back at the beginning of the two paths.

I moved along the left hand path, which was not as easy to travel as the other had been, and yet there were no obstacles that couldn't be overcome.

As I got further along, I saw a figure standing in the path. It was neither male nor female and was formed out of coruscating silver and gold light and expressed a sense of prosperity. The figure held out in its right hand a beautiful, ripe, red apple.

I took the apple and ate it.

When I reflected on the vision, I believed that the bowl of fruit told me to not believe everything I saw, as what was presented could be a trap.

The ripe apple told me to take only what I needed and God would watch over me. The silver and gold light was the female and male aspects of Divinity in harmonious union. They told me that to be in harmony with myself, that in seeking balance, prosperity and abundance would be drawn into my life.

As always, one path was beneficial, and one was not. As always, I was free to choose which to take.

The silver bowl and the ripe fruit told me to be aware of illusion, as greed could be presented as plentiful and wholesome.

To me, the other path looked much more interesting. There were mysteries there.

With this vision on my mind, I went for a coffee by the waterfront. As I walked toward the café, a man approached saying, "Just invite Jesus into your life and you will be saved."

I wondered what he would have done if Jesus turned up in his lounge room? What would he have done if Jesus came to him in visions? How would he handle being asked to write a book by Jesus, Uriel and other angels? Would he think he was crazy as I had thought I was?

And that night, I dreamt the strangest dream.

An ark sailed across the red sand dunes of the Australian desert. There was no water; the ark slid across sand. Time passed and a door opened in the ark's side and out came all manner of birds and animals to populate the land.

Men and women emerged from the ark and planted trees and shrubs. The rains came and soon the land that was once desert became fertile and abundant.

That dream spoke to me of my spiritual growth and told me that once barren ground would soon become fertile and abundant.

Then *he* came back again, turning up in another vision.

Jesus stood on barren ground. Behind him grew a few stunted trees and bushes, all struggling to survive and competing for nutrients and moisture.

Floating in the air above Jesus was a symbol made up of a cross and trefoil harmoniously entwined within a circle. The circle was yellow, the trefoil blue and the cross was red.

Spoken words accompanied the symbol. *"Not alone through the female aspect of Divinity, nor alone through the male; only through the harmonious union of the two shall humanity prevail."*

My gaze moved back down to Jesus and where it had been only him when I first looked, now Mary Magdalene stood at his side holding his hand and beside each of them holding their other hands, was a child. A girl held Mary's hand and a boy, Jesus' hand.

Jesus wore full-length priestly robes of blood red, and an ankle length sky blue vest. Mary was wearing the complimentary opposite, with her full-length robe sky blue and her ankle length vest blood red. They were the male and female aspects of Divinity.

The girl holding Mary's hand was named Sarah, and the boy, a couple of years older than her, was Tomas. Both were dressed in ankle length white robes.

An Archangel's Gift

From beneath their feet, what was dry and cracked earth moistened and darkened. Worms moved in the soil as it became fertile and seeds began to sprout.

Grass began to grow and kissed their feet. Trees flowed out of the ground and forests appeared with birds and animals aplenty.

All this happened beginning where Jesus, Mary, Sarah and Tomas stood, and exploded forward while behind them, the landscape was still barren, cracked and dry.

Jesus had shown me where I had come from spiritually, and where I was going.

The words I heard told me that to be in harmony, I needed to acknowledge both the female and male aspects of Divinity within myself. It showed me that Mary Magdalene was Jesus complimentary opposite and his equal. Together they represented the male and female aspects of Divinity in harmony.

To encourage myself to talk about my visions, which I was reluctant to do for a long time, I had the symbol that floated above Jesus and Mary in the vision tattooed on my forearms to encourage people to ask me what they meant. I also had the words from the vision added to the tattoos in runes outside of the circle.

Chapter 25
Not Dead Again?

I spent a lot of time debating with myself whether or not to include the following, as I felt embarrassed when I listed all of the things that had happened. It was a long list.

I had just about decided to leave out the times when Spirit intervened in my life and saved it, when Archangel Mickhael suggested I include them, so here are some of them.

While I was in Melbourne, the weather was miserable, cold and rainy, as it could be there. I had come out of the library and was standing amongst the crowd at the traffic lights waiting for them to change.

Tucked up in my windcheater with the hood up, I stared through the rain at the lights across the road. As they changed to green for *walk*, I stepped off the gutter putting all of my weight into my leading foot when I was frozen in place.

Even though my weight to my lead foot and my forward motion were both committed, I was somehow stationary with my right foot suspended, mid-stride, six inches above the surface of the road.

There was no sensation of being stopped but stopped I most definitely was.

In that instant, a bus ran a red light and passed within inches of my face. The water sprayed up by the bus didn't touch me.

As soon as the bus passed I was released and allowed to cross the road with the rest of the crowd. Head down, shoulders hunched, I was embarrassed that I had been saved, again. Is it that I was clumsy, or unobservant, or what?

When I got home, I sat down, took a deep breath, and asked. *Why does this happen to me? Why do other people get killed and I get saved? What does it mean? Is there something wrong with me? Have I done something wrong?*

Blind panic swirled around my mind as I thought of all the times I had been saved by Spirit…*Why?*

Whenever I set out to write down my list of times I had been *saved,* I got embarrassed.

I wondered why being saved from death embarrassed me.

What did it say about me, that I had been saved so many times? I didn't think I wanted to know the answer.

I felt like I didn't have the ability to describe how being saved again and again felt…it went beyond my understanding…it was confusing as it broke all the rules I had been taught as to how reality worked…I would like to have had the words and the skill to convey my experiences and the emotions they evoked. There were times when Spirit physically intervened in my world and there were times when my physical world was affected in a way that, according to the rules I was taught, should have been impossible.

If this was all going to be written down, despite my reservations, I suppose the most prominent experience, was the time I was saved from being killed by a falling brick wall when I was laying bricks for a living, several years before the car accident.

It had been raining all week and the bricks were saturated with water making them heavier than usual. The wall was almost as high as I could reach, with only one course of bricks to go.

Two other bricklayers worked on the scaffold with me that day; one at each end with me in the middle. I stood between the wall and a stack of bricks about three feet long and as high as my waist.

Then, as my two workmates moved to their ends of the wall to put the string line up, the wall fell.

I saw it fall toward me; then I was looking at it from about seven or eight feet away. I was standing on the safety rail holding onto the upright with my left hand, my trowel still grasped in my right. The other two were just past their ends of the wall and, when the wall fell, they immediately leapt forward and began throwing bricks from the pile of rubble to dig me out.

But I wasn't there. It took me several attempts to attract their attention as they had seen the wall fall on me. Or at least, fall where I had been.

When I finally got their attention, they both looked bewildered seeing me up on the safety rail unharmed. Neither they, nor I, ever mentioned anything about what had happened.

As the wall fell, somehow I was moved out of harm's way. I should have been killed and yet there I was standing on the safety rail, three feet above the deck and about seven or eight feet away.

How? Why? I felt embarrassed…and a little guilty that I wasn't lying mangled under that pile of bricks…not to mention scared because what just happened was impossible, *wasn't it?*

Twice, I fell through faulty scaffolding only to be suddenly standing safely on the ground below without a scratch. What I mean is that I began to fall, and then was moved to safety.

The first time was early in my apprenticeship. I had just built a scaffold and planked it out with new six metre hardwood planks. Having completed my task, I walked along the planks to check my work and at a point about halfway between supports, I stood on a large knot in one of the planks. The plank gave way and I fell, or started to fall, before I was suddenly on the ground beneath the scaffold.

My first reaction was to look around to see if anyone had seen what had happened, then to sigh with relief that no one had. I felt like a kid getting caught with his hand in the cookie jar, like I had been doing something I was not supposed to be doing.

That one probably wouldn't have killed me although if I had passed through the planks as would be expected, I would have broken my legs or crushed my pelvis.

A couple of months later, I was on the same site early on a cold frosty winter's morning. I was, as was my habit, climbing up the outside of the scaffold rather than using the stairs as I was supposed to—I did like to climb stuff.

The steel poles and cross beams had patches of ice which I carefully managed to avoid until I got to about the fourth floor level. I reached for the next horizontal bar and grabbed hold of ice-covered steel and when I went to take my weight, both my hands slipped before my feet were set and I fell.

But I wasn't falling. I was moved horizontally onto the next plank deck of the scaffold that I should have fallen past on my way to the ground.

Something, or someone, moved me and saved me from falling to my death. Somehow I was taken from my fall and placed safely on the deck and it was done so fast there was no sensation of movement.

I was falling and then I wasn't.

I took a deep breath and held onto the nearest scaffold pole, my heart racing. After another couple of deep breaths, I stepped off the scaffold onto the concrete floor of the building then made my way, slowly and cautiously, down the stairs, holding tight to the handrail the whole way down.

Once I got to the bottom, I walked away from the building a little then turned and looked up at where I had slipped.

I don't know how long I stood and stared before the foreman came over and stood beside me and said, "I saw you fall. You should be dead."

He was quiet for a while, and then turned his head toward me and asked, "What are you thinking?" He pointed up to where I had slipped.

I looked at the scaffolding and said, "I have to climb back up there or I will never get on another scaffold as long as I live."

He was thoughtful for two or three breaths, stroked his chin with his hand. "I understand," was all he said.

I took a deep breath, walked over to the bottom of the scaffold, and climbed it carefully.

I fell through the scaffold another time, although we were working on a house rather than a five-storey building.

The scaffold was different to the one used when the wall fell, which was steel framed and steel planked where everything clicked together. This one was made from steel frames with cross braces and wooden planks, similar to the other one I fell through.

I had just climbed up onto the scaffold after throwing bricks up to my boss. As I walked along the planks toward where I would be working, I stepped onto a spot where the ends of two planks met in mid-air. That was definitely a no-no when building scaffold, as that point would hold no weight at all. I stepped on that spot and the support beneath me gave way. The scaffold was twelve feet high and suddenly I was standing on the ground below. My feet were placed neatly in the only spot not occupied by pieces of broken brick. My boss yelled at me for standing on that spot and I yelled back. "Who's the idiot that put those planks there?"

An Archangel's Gift

It took a bit more yelling at each other and a little bit of time before he admitted that he was the idiot that put those planks there.

On that same site with the scaffold the same height but on another wall and on another day, I was up on the scaffold, which ran along the side of the house, just around the corner from where I fell through. I had been catching bricks and loading up the scaffold, which was ready for us to start laying bricks straight after morning tea.

I was the apprentice in this gang, made up of two bricklayers, a labourer and me.

I was still up on the scaffold as the other three sat down with their backs to the site shed when the scaffold collapsed in front of them. It had been raining a lot. The ground was saturated and unstable and although we could not tell by walking on it, it couldn't take the weight of the scaffold.

The scaffold ran along the full length of that part of the house and just outside the scaffold sat a delivery of bricks, a delivery of sand and a delivery of timber. They were positioned parallel to the house and scaffold, so when the scaffold came down, it fell on the bricks, sand and timber. I was still on the scaffold when it fell.

As I walked out of the dust, stepping carefully amongst the rubble from the fallen scaffold, my boss and the other two were standing staring open mouthed at me with the same look that the two bricklayers had when the wall fell and I wasn't under it.

I walked over, sat down, poured myself a cup of tea and lit a cigarette while staring at the mess all over the ground in front of me.

The other three sat down again, mouths still hanging open.

My boss tried to take a sip of his coffee but couldn't hold the cup still, spilling it on his hand and leg. He put down his cup and tried to light a cigarette but his hands were shaking too much so I lit it for him. He kept looking at me and shaking his head. He couldn't say anything for a while. A couple of minutes passed and then he looked at me, shook his head and said. "God! Your hands aren't even shaking."

I held my right hand up parallel to the ground at eye height. *Huh! Steady as a rock.*

It was different for me than it had been for them.

By the reactions of my colleagues, for them the scaffold had fallen fast, while for me it was slow and a little dreamlike with plenty of time to get off safely.

As the scaffold began to collapse, I was standing opposite the delivery of bricks, which I didn't fancy falling onto while riding a collapsing scaffold.

The outside legs of the scaffold collapsed into the ground causing the scaffold to fall outwards away from the house.

An Archangel's Gift

As the scaffold began to move a strange feeling of calm washed through my body. It was palpable and a bit difficult to describe in words.

As it fell in slow motion, I walked along the scaffold until I reached the spot opposite the sand and waited; it seemed to be awhile. I waited until the scaffold was about halfway to the ground then I pushed off in a dive toward the sand pile, tucked into a forward roll down the back slope of the sand, stood up, and walked over to where the other three were standing open mouthed, sat down and poured myself a cup of tea.

That was the first time it felt like *time* was looking out for me; like time didn't want me to get hurt.

Just writing that down felt weird and yet that was only the first time it happened to me.

The second time, I was no longer an apprentice. I was married and had a young son.

By then, I was working for myself subcontracting and also working by myself. I had just finished loading the scaffold with mortar and bricks and was about to start laying bricks to the gable end of the house when a weld on one of the steel trestles in the scaffolding broke with a loud bang and the entire scaffold collapsed.

A builder who I worked for from time to time was working on the next house. He was close enough to where I was working, however, to hold a conversation.

Within a couple of seconds of the scaffold collapsing, he was in amongst the rubble frantically throwing aside six metre long planks like they weighed nothing and flipping bricks aside trying to dig me out from under the bricks, mortar, mortar boards, wooden planks and steel trestles.

And yet again, I wasn't there.

When I heard the weld break, it was pretty loud. I was standing at the right hand end of the scaffold and again I felt that strange sense of calm wash through me. I felt it through every cell of my body and it felt a little like standing under a shower except that I could feel it inside as well as outside just as I had last time that *time* had slowed down for me.

I walked slowly and calmly along the scaffold feeling like I had all the time in the world until I got about three quarters of the way along, reached up with my left hand and wrapped my fingers over the barge board at the edge of the roof.

Again it took quite a bit of effort to get my rescuer to understand that I wasn't under that pile of rubble. His stunned face looked up at me, down at the rubble, then up at me again, his head shaking from side to side.

As I was hanging from the roof by my left hand he went and got a ladder, climbed up onto the roof and pulled me up.

Looking around while I was up there, I saw that the roof tiling was finished except for one small spot about three inches wide and one tile long. This was the only place on the end of the roof where I could have held on and it was on the opposite side to where I was when the scaffold collapsed.

Having just gone through some of those times Spirit saved me, and having been told by Archangel Mickhael that, in the war between Light and Dark, the Light cannot act without Dark having acted first. Therefore, if I followed that train of thought, it meant that Spirit could only act to save me because darkness had acted first to cause me harm.

When I thought about all the times I was saved, I realised how protective my spiritual guardians were. It seemed I had my own personal spiritual bodyguards.

Chapter 26
A Grey Streetscape

I was restless. Half a dozen tasks were started and left undone. I put on some music; turned it off. I switched on the television; turned that off. I paced around the house, settled down to read and stopped without finishing the first line. I went outside onto the grass, lay in the sun and looked up at the crisp blue autumn sky.

Archangel Mickhael had told me that from confusion came clarity and I thought about it there on the grass. I also thought about the ways I blocked myself with excuses not to do what I was supposed to be doing. Then I saw this vision.

I stood on a path before a vertical barrier of flood debris. There were rocks, clay, sticks and logs all forming an impenetrable wall before my eyes. I was so close, I could touch the debris and I knew these were the blockages I had created in my past that would affect my future.

To the left, the wall continued on as far as I could see and I knew I couldn't get around it that way. I also knew that I could not climb over the wall, through the wall or go under it. Luckily for me, the path I was on went to the right and only a few paces in front of me, a river had carved a path through the wall and once past it, the path followed the river. I took the path around the wall and followed it along the river.

I understood that if I followed the path I was supposed to take, the obstacles would be washed away. I received more positive encouragement that I should continue on this path.

Not long after, I saw a vision of myself standing alone in an empty street that ran straight off into the distance before me. That was the path I was on.

The colour scheme was like a black and white photograph. It was a two-lane bitumen street with concrete kerbs and a concrete footpath along both sides. The street was lined with the backs of buildings between one and three storeys tall with no windows on any of the ground floors. It was the back street of a minor industrial area and all the doors, windows and gates were locked or barred. High fences with barbed wire framed the buildings that weren't connected, and the fences were covered so nothing could be seen through them.

I looked down the empty street and felt depressed.
Is this what I have to look forward to for the rest of my life?

I looked up at the building beside me, then back down to the street.

My way forward was blocked.

I noticed a green safety fence, like the ones they put around swimming pools, running from building to building about twenty yards before me. Standing on my side of the fence was a fourteen-foot tall Archangel Uriel. His wings were spread and they stretched easily from the buildings on one side of the street to the other. He had his arms stretched out as though to block my path.

Standing in front of Uriel was a six-foot Jesus who also had his arms spread, blocking my path.

Both Uriel and Jesus indicated with their right hands and turned their heads to look at the side of the street to my left.

I looked and saw that there was a gap in one of the buildings, like a hole from a wrecking-ball that had left a pile of rubble on the ground. Both Uriel and Jesus directed me toward this opening and encouraged me to enter.

I did.

The other side was a different world. I saw lush green grass and trees in the distance. Standing on a grassy hillside not far into that reality was a woman wearing a white cheesecloth dress; she was waiting for me.

As I looked at this vision, both the visions of my *lifeline* and *Follow the earthen cascade* slid in and lined up with it, one atop the other.

The hole in the wall lined up with both my time of tumultuous confusion shown in my lifeline vision, and the rock in *Follow the earthen cascade*. This also caused the new direction in my lifeline vision, and the path beyond the fence in *Follow the earthen cascade*, to line up perfectly with the woman in white positioned on the path.

Simply put, I understood that when I finished my book I would have no choice but to take that new path, and on that path, I would meet the woman that was waiting for me.

The vision also told me that the three visions were interconnected. My time of tumultuous confusion was also the time I spent writing this book and that was what caused the hole in the wall.

Another vision followed.

As had often happened before, for a short time everything I saw was chaotic, and then a picture formed amongst the swirling background and slowly moved closer and became more distinct.

I saw the ancient dried up body of a mummy. The skin was brittle, grey, covered in dust but intact.

A rustling noise came from within the mummy, a scratching like dry leaves rustling in the wind, but sharper.

As I watched, the mouth of the mummy opened wide and a seemingly endless stream of locusts swarmed out.

I was then drawn back until I could see planet Earth before me, like a picture taken from a space station in orbit.

The planet was in darkness until a spark of light appeared on the horizon. The spark was the mummy and as the locusts fanned out, they began to consume the darkness until soon the entire planet was bathed in Light.

As I looked at the vision, I connected the vision with the prophecy carved into my staff.

1:1 *In the days that number nine,*
1:2 *from the New World will arise*, ***the prophet Elijah**,*
1:3 ***to bring forth and unfurl the Faith of the One,***
1:4 ***to express the word of Divinity**,*
1:5 *at a time when darkness and light*
1:6 *fight for dominance in the world of man.*

The ancient dried up body was ***the prophet Elijah.***

The locusts swarming from his mouth to consume darkness were—***to bring forth and unfurl the faith of the One, to express the Word of Divinity...***

An Archangel's Gift

Chapter 27

Sitting in a Forest Clearing

I took myself out into the forest and found a nice clearing. There, I drifted into meditation and found myself sitting on a rock beside a path, on the side of a barren mountain. My staff rested on the rock beside me.

As I sat, a traveller approached out of the mist from the direction I was headed and paused in his journey. Leaning on his staff, he looked at me, took the few steps necessary and sat down on the rock about three or four feet from me. He laid his staff down between us; the red painted runes that spiralled around it glistened in the sunlight. He offered to share his meal with me as, he noted, I had none.

I drank some of his wine, and ate some of his bread and cheese. We ate in silence, enjoying the meal.

Once we finished, he took up his staff and, leaning on it as though to get up, he turned his head to me and asked, "How goes your journey?"

Puzzled by the question I replied. "Sometimes frustrating, at other times confusing. There seems to be only one path and following it makes little sense to me."

With a small movement of his head, he indicated the mountain behind us and said. "Climb to the top of this mountain and your path will be much clearer before you. Climb to the top of this mountain, and you will find what you're looking for."

I turned to look up at the mountain and thought, *Yes, I can climb that without too much trouble.*

I turned back to the traveller and it was as though he had never been there at all. He was gone.

I began to climb the mountain while thinking about my visitor. He seemed to know me and where I was on my journey. A man who carried a staff, which, every time I looked at it, the runes carved into it had a different configuration.

Ah! I caught my breath, I realised that he was wearing sandals, and those I remembered.

Eventually I reached the summit. With both hands wrapped around my staff, I leant on it and I looked out at what lay before me. I noted that the runes carved into my own staff had reconfigured themselves.

The traveller was suddenly beside me, leaning on his staff in that familiar way and looking out at what lay before me. "Tell me what you see," he whispered.

I took a moment then replied. "I see a land full of dangers and pitfalls. I see a path cut by lava flows and flooding rivers. I see broken bridges across yawning chasms. I see dark forests inhabited with creatures that would drink my blood and send my soul into damnation. And beyond all this I see a castle high up on a mountaintop, my destination, seemingly impossible to get to. That's what I see."

The traveller nodded. "Good, now come with me."

Instantly, we were back where we had shared our meal but the mountainside was no longer barren. It was enfolded in a magnificent forest inhabited by dragons and unicorns, elves and elementals. Then, in the blink of an eye, we were back on the mountaintop, and the landscape I saw earlier was gone. The change was almost beyond explanation.

I turned to the traveller. A little amused, he said. "See what a difference your perceptions of reality can have on the world you choose to inhabit."

Before me, the landscape was now green and filled with friendly forests; the slow flowing shallow rivers could be easily crossed. There were open grasslands and clear paths. The castle, that had before seemed to be unreachable, had a clear path to it.

I looked to the traveller and realisation slowly dawned. The staff he was leaning on was the staff I was leaning on. The sandals on his feet were the sandals on my feet.

He was me; a future me, as he had come down the path that I had been walking up, and he had come out of the mist. It seemed that I had been making my path difficult simply because I thought it was difficult. I was invited to change that by changing the way I looked at my path.

On New Year's Eve, Sybil, Jayson and I decided to move to Queensland, so I sorted through things to take and things to throw away, which brought me to my guns. I had two black powder rifles until that day when I broke them up and threw them in the garbage.

I hadn't fired them since I shot a kangaroo that spoke to me back in 1992. I know how that sounds: impossible. But that is what happened.

I had been shooting on Mum and Dad's farm when I shot a large male kangaroo but did not kill him. He asked clearly in my mind. *"Why did you kill me?"*

That ended my hunting days.

I really didn't want to write about him as, describing how I felt, took me back into that deeply emotional experience. But then, I owed it to the one I killed.

I'd killed animals before but this nearly sent me over the edge; kangaroos were not supposed to talk inside your mind.

I remembered going numb with shock.

I had to ask my hunting partner to finish him off; I just couldn't do it. He was in pain and dying and I even had trouble finding my voice to ask.

I was affected terribly for days after as the implications of the event sunk into my awareness.

A kangaroo spoke to me.

How is that possible?

It felt, I felt, terrible. My immediate reaction was: *Oh God, I've murdered him.*

My heart sobbed for him as I grieved for a soul I never knew.

His question spoke of an awareness I would not have been able to imagine before I shot him but he was no different to me: a soul trying to live his life the best way he knew how when I cut it short.

That was twenty years ago and I can still see pain in his eyes and hear his voice.

I hope my life, in some small way, eventually makes up for taking his.

It seemed that I had been delegated to find us somewhere to live in Brisbane, so I went out and bought myself a Brisbane street directory and started cancelling out places not to live. For a start we all wanted to live near the ocean so that simplified it.

When I looked at the maps, the first thing I noticed was that there was an oil refinery and a sewage treatment plant on the south side of the river, which encouraged me to look north of the river.

Immediately north was the Brisbane Airport, so we needed to go far enough north to be away from the noise.

North of the airport were Shorncliffe, Sandgate and Brighton; then about three kilometres of bridge across the bay led to the Redcliffe Peninsula with the suburbs of Woody Point, Clontarf, Margate, Redcliffe, Scarborough and Kippa-Ring. Then a little further north was Deception Bay.

After a bit of discussion, Jayson and I flew up to have a look about Redcliffe and Deception Bay. We undertook a two-day scouting trip and found a house to rent; and we also found the trees I saw in a vision and drew in September the previous year, making it feel like the right place.

While I recorded the vision of the trees, I saw another vision of myself walking along a narrow pathway winding its way between two tall cliffs. The path was narrow but wide enough for me to walk comfortably between the two cliff faces.

At one point, there was a huge mass of stone overhanging the path and it was scary to walk under it, but I continued along the path as that was the way I had to go.

Once past that point, the landscape opened and softened. The cliffs became rounded hills and trees and shrubs lined the path instead of cliffs. Around the next bend, I looked out over a beautiful green valley with a river running through the centre. This place held no fear or feelings of being restricted like it felt on the path before the overhanging rocks. This place held an invitation and a promise: a promise of something I couldn't express.

This place made me want to run and jump, and skip and sing. I would not have been surprised if I had seen elves and fairies, unicorns and dragons as I strolled through those trees.

What does it mean?

As soon as I asked, I heard the answer in my mind. *"Your path is clear and safe with some illusory obstacles before you. The cliffs you thought brooding and dangerous are there to protect you. The overhanging rocks represent your fears. Once you have moved beyond those fears you will come to a place that evokes a magickal sense and energy to the world around you. This is a place where magick happens."*

An Archangel's Gift

South-East Queensland

2005 to 2016

An Archangel's Gift

Chapter 28

Just a Distraction

It was July 2005 and three of the intrepid explorers who had left Canberra all those years ago were now in Redcliffe, a small city situated on Moreton Bay north of Brisbane. We thought we were moving to Brisbane but quickly found out we were wrong.

The winter chill felt warm to me as I was not yet acclimated to the subtropical climate, so I had decided to go down to Redcliffe Pier and enjoy the bay. As I sat there, watching the sunrise over the lapping waves, I had a strong premonition that my world was about to get a lot bigger. I wasn't really sure what that meant, but that's what I felt.

It was a nice, calm day. The water was beautiful and blue and as I was staring at the horizon, I had a vision that I was sitting in a lounge room and across from me was my future self.

I was both there then, and at a place in the future when this book was complete. My future aspect was studying two versions of my work. In one hand, he held the finished book open, while in the other he had the book as it stood in 2005. My future self showed me what I still had left to do, and pointed out sections that needed to be revised.

This felt weird, in that I was trying to hold onto multiple perceptions of reality and let them go at the same time. It felt like I was struggling, pushing and pulling inside my brain. It gave me a headache.

Once I had settled into Redcliffe, I began to get more insistent messages to write my book. I couldn't ignore the voice inside my head that said. *"Write your book. Write your book. How's your book going? How's your book going?"*

When I asked what was supposed to go in this book, I was insistently told that it was my choice, which was still stressful and scary. I thought it would have been bad enough trying to write a book with what Jesus asked me to write, but giving me the choice of what I wrote freaked me out even more. He wanted me to write about myself and if I did that, I wouldn't have been able to hide anymore. But then again I asked myself, how else would I undertake a journey into self-awareness?

So I began to sort through my diaries and think about what I could write. I looked at what Jesus had taught me. I read through all my notes and diaries looking for the best way to fill the pages. I felt nervous but decided I had the courage to take this leap of faith. My journey into self-awareness deepened.

Edward Spellman

It was a Saturday night and I had just gotten some advice from Archangel Mickhael. *"Define yourself, Edward, by the fact that you have been, and are always, touched by the Divine; touched by angels, that you are being guided and protected every second of every day, and every day to come. Define yourself by your experiences with Jesus, Uriel, Running Wolf, the horseman and Farronell. The paradigm that controls and runs this world is about to change. Look at your life as challenges not failures. Pride is good; do not let it become arrogance. Look at everything that you have overcome and be amazed at what you have overcome."*

I asked Mickhael about something I was working on in my workshop. I can't remember the question exactly, as the answer he gave me pushed it from my mind.

Mickhael said. *"Anything you do that is not your book is just a distraction. At this time, your path is to write your book. And remember, Edward: failure is not failure. When an obstacle comes to you it is an expression of the universe's faith in you, and it is an opportunity to lead you toward your ultimate destiny. If there were no obstacles, you would not be on the correct path."*

An Archangel's Gift

Chapter 29
Not That Way

At the nursing home where I worked, there were a group of my fellow workmates I called 'the hyenas' because they ganged up on and attacked people at their weakest.

One day, they were giving one of the women there a hard time, so I tried to negate a bit of their negativity. I said hello and asked how her day was going. She was from a Spanish-speaking country so I asked how to say hello and good morning in Spanish. She asked if she could be my friend and I said. "Of course you can."

After a couple of weeks of bantering in the corridors at work she asked me to come to a barbeque, and I decided to go even though I was focused on my writing and not interested in pursuing any relationships then.

Once I got to the barbeque her behaviour changed and I discovered her perception of a friend was very different to mine.

Being wary, I asked my guides what would happen if I allowed her to get as close to me as she seemed to want and I saw this vision.

I was standing on a natural stone platform. The rock beneath my feet was solid but I was standing near the edge. Immediately before me there was a vortex of dark energy like a whirlpool of thunderclouds. Sticking out of the vortex were three straight vertical branches with sharp thorns facing downward at a forty-five degree angle. The branches looked like telephone poles and were the colour of young rose shoots. They did not move but the vortex swirled around them and I knew that if I took a step closer I would be pulled into the raging storm and torn to bits.

Standing on the stone shelf showed me I was safe where I was. On seeing that vortex, I immediately excused myself, knowing that to continue my association with her would be akin to stepping into the vortex and being ripped to shreds.

I was wondering about the vision of the vortex when another came, another warning. This time I saw a road paved with broken bottles and all the jagged bits faced up. I was standing barefoot at the end of the road, just before the broken glass.

The visions gave me pause to think about what the woman might want from me. I told her that I do not want to stay in contact and asked her to please stop calling, texting and e-mailing as I was not interested.

It felt like the right thing to do, both for me and for her. I didn't tell her about the vision that said my emotional self would be shredded as though I had walked barefoot down a road paved with broken bottles.

While I didn't understand why I saw those warnings, I was happy I did. It seemed I was being shown which path was beneficial to me and which was not. I had learned to trust my guidance by then and stopped questioning needlessly.

Maybe that was what Jesus and Mickhael meant about taking a leap of faith?

Around the same time, a friend of a friend asked me to do some work for her. She wanted me to do the fit out on a little shop that was her latest venture.

Tired of working in the nursing home, I seriously considered doing it, as two weeks with pay away from aged care sounded good.

I took my time considering whether or not the opportunity was viable for me. As I was contemplating the pros and cons, I had a vision of a very large and nasty steel trap; a wolf trap.

The wolf that the trap was set to catch was Running Wolf and as I was him, I really didn't want to step into that one, so I told her. "Thanks, but I can't do the job."

She called and tried to convince me that the job would be good for me as well as for her but while she was talking, I saw another vision. This time I was an archery target with an archer getting ready to shoot. It was a simple vision and I knew not to take the job, no matter how much she tried to convince me otherwise.

I respectfully declined as these two visions just told me that if I were to take on the job it would be a trap and make me a target. How, I didn't know, but that didn't matter. I trusted my guidance.

Chapter 30
Spiritual Amnesia and Confusion

I had another message from Jesus. *"Trust other people's expertise."*

I knew I could be a bit of a don't-trust-other-people-with-my-pet-projects sort of a person, so I would have to remember this piece of advice, and allow other people's expertise through my defences. As I would learn, that wasn't easy for my little control freak self.

It was growing clearer that something was missing inside of me.

I was in a car accident when I was sixteen when a doctor put thirty stitches in my head. After the wound healed, whenever I got bumped or hit the scar, I lost my memory.

It was almost always the same, I would lose two years, and it would take anywhere from a few hours to a couple of days for those memories to come back. Although, there were still some holes in my memory where things did not return and I saw there were spaces in my mind that were blank.

After several years and a few more bumps on the head, I recognised the amnesia as it happened because I could remember an earlier event, as the amnesia always took two years from me, and I could remember before that.

I didn't know how to write this so it wasn't confusing because frankly, it was very confusing but I gave it my best shot.

It bent my mind into knots and challenged my perceptions of reality as well as what I had been taught in how my perceptions of reality should be.

I realised that having a hole in my mind was something that could be felt. I could feel the space where the missing memories were supposed to be and I could feel them slide back in just as if I were sliding a DVD or a book back into its spot on the shelf.

Although losing my memory hadn't happened to me for years, I still felt there was something missing within me. It wasn't the same as the amnesia I'd had so many times before; it was different somehow. This time it felt like it was on another level of my being. It felt like I had some kind of spiritual amnesia.

It just felt wrong. Something inside of me was trying to find its way out and my ego and fear were trying to keep it buried. It was a bit like playing hide and seek with a spiritual concept I knew was on the tip of my consciousness but I just couldn't bring it into my conscious awareness. I guessed I just wasn't ready yet.

I had been thinking about writing this book and, at the same time, being afraid to write it. I kept asking myself why I should write it.

I drifted off to sleep with those thoughts running through my mind and when I woke in the early hours of the morning, I saw a particularly powerful vision. It was one of those things that felt like it would send me right round the twist, if I wasn't already there!

I saw myself standing behind the barred window of a stone cell. My fingers were bleeding from scrabbling at the bars and my voice was hoarse from screaming. *Let me out of here!*

Behind me on the far side of the cell, the door stood wide open and led to my workshop. I heard the words. *"The key to your freedom is in your workshop; all you have to do is turn around."*

I asked Jesus through Archangel Mickhael about this. He answered. *"When the son becomes one, the child within will blend the three, all shall see the moon as one, and one will become all as one."*

I had no idea what that meant but I knew that Jesus liked to give me puzzles.

With all that going through my mind again and again, I sat down to meditate to try and quieten it all down.

As my mind drifted away on a current of nothingness, I saw myself underwater in the ocean. I tumbled under the waves of a dark stormy sea, with no control and no idea which way was up or down.

Before long, I saw the light and headed for it.

Then, all of a sudden, I was sitting cross-legged on top of a calm sea, bathing in the sunlight and drifting with the current. I was like a floating yogi, which is interesting because I usually find sitting cross-legged uncomfortable. A sense of relief, calm and satisfaction flowed through me. I felt the soft warmth of the sun flow through my body and I was at peace.

Relief!

At least, even though I was still totally confused, I knew I would get through this and with that assurance, my mind calmed down.

Chapter 31
Your Past Points to Your Path

I had my palm read and the reader told me that I would write a book and that I was protected. He also told me there was another female partner coming into my life.

I thought it would be interesting to see if I would allow a woman to get that close to me again; I hadn't since my last break up. I felt a bit skittish on that front but wondered if he was talking about the woman in the white cheesecloth dress.

Three weeks later, while I was out having coffee with a friend, a vision appeared that I could not interpret. I decided to create a three-dimensional version from wood, leather and inks.

When I finished recreating this vision in the physical world, I called it *The Prophecy Shield* because it predicted the future and as I hung it on my workshop wall, the feelings I had were inexplicable. It touched me deeply.

An Archangel's Gift

Below is a photo of *The Prophecy Shield* and my growing understanding of its symbolism.

The shield was 1200mm wide and convex in shape with a 120mm rise, so it was a segment of a sphere.

The footprints told me; *you are never alone. I am always by your side*, words that felt like spring sunshine on my skin.

The line made of what looks like dominos was a timeline and it said: *In conjunction with the symbols gathered behind it and around the edge of the shield, that at a specific point in time, I would see much more detail in the visions I had seen, and the ones I would see in the future.*

The paths of dotted lines that meander and criss-cross from the bottom to the top of the shield had me thinking for a while until Mickhael asked me to highlight the four positive paths forward for humanity.

Having followed his instruction, I stood back and looked at it for a while. There were twenty-three paths set out across the prophecy shield and Archangel Mickhael had told me that four of them were positive and beneficial to humanity and Mother Earth. That meant that the other nineteen paths were not beneficial either for the planet or for us.

As I sat and looked at the shield, I began to see the twenty-three paths as streams of energy. The four positive and beneficial paths that I highlighted were five times the width of the negative paths. As I allowed my mind to wander, the paths began to flow and every time a negative path crossed a positive, it picked up a little of that positive energy and was not as dark as it had been before. Every negative path crossed again and again over a positive so that the negative, once they had crossed enough times, completely changed their nature to one that was positive and beneficial.

The Prophecy Shield by Edward Spellman, 2016.

An Archangel's Gift

I had the shield set up so that as I worked at my computer, it was always there, encouraging me to keep going.

I was sitting at my computer working on this book when I saw a vision of myself sitting in a cave high up on the side of a mountain. I was sitting on a funny shaped stool with my legs tucked under me and I was wearing a brown monk's robe like the Franciscans, and I was pen in hand, working on my book. Soon, I finished the book, stood up and took off the robe. I turned around and walked out of the cave.

I felt I was being encouraged to be a little hermit-like and spend some time just working on this project.

Shortly after this vision, I had the opportunity to ask Archangel Samhael about it. "Is there anything you could tell me about the vision I had of me as a monk in a mountain cave?"

Samhael said. *"Being disconnected from all human beings besides your core group allows you to realise and link to your power. You must replenish in nature. It is vital to your sanity, to your power and to your future. And Edward, know that visions are rare. How rare? Big time rare, most people do not have the backbone to deal with them."*

Again, and again, I heard. *"The key to your freedom is in your workshop."*

Finally I understood. As I was meant to be delving into myself, the workshop in question was internal, so what it meant was, *the key to your freedom is within you.*

Not long after that, Mickhael gave me a message. He said. *"Edward, I have a message for you from Jesus. He wants you to know that your past points to your path."*

"Thank you." I said. That bent my head a little bit and almost gave me frown lines trying to work it out.

I thought, *What past? This life? A past life? Before the accident? After the accident?*

I just left it for a while until, while cleaning up my manuscript, I got to this point and heard a question in my mind. *"What were you writing about before you got to here?"*

"That's easy. Visions, dreams, prophecy, my past…oh!"

"My past points to my path, doesn't it?"

That would be the same path that was shown in the vision *Follow the earthen cascade,* which means that once this book is finished, my path will be one of visions, dreams, prophecy, and writing about them. Although without the *tumultuous confusion,* as that ends when this book is finished and the path beyond the fence is clear.

An Archangel's Gift

Chapter 32
The Holy Spirit as a Dove

The sense that something was missing inside of me was persistent. I went looking for it and only found where it wasn't. Still, I felt something coming and I was impatient.

To help me express how I felt, I went out and bought two A4 size picture frames, along with some green, red and black paint. I pulled the frames apart, painted my hands green and pressed them against the glass leaving my handprints on them. I then painted over that with black paint. When that dried, I scratched two parallel lines in the black paint framing my handprints and painted those red. I finished the frames by painting them black to match the background.

The finished pieces expressed how I had been feeling, with my hands on the other side of the glass in darkness. Creating that bit of art was a therapeutic and amazing way of expressing something in visual terms that I could not verbalise. Whenever I looked at those pieces, I realised that I had felt as though I was locked away in the dark with no way out and no way to express it.

Mickhael said to me. *"Edward, you need to be able to accept things that most people believe are impossible."*

Hmmm! Why would he say that? I wondered.

He knew everything that had happened to me. He knew that much of it was what most people believed impossible.

Nothing was ever as simple as it seemed with archangels, however. There was always more than one layer to what they had to say.

While talking about accepting things that most people would believe are impossible, I saw a vision of the Holy Spirit as a white dove flapping its wings. Every time the wings flapped, the dove got smaller and closer until eventually it flew into the centre of my chest and took up residence there.

The Holy Spirit flew into my heart to heal it and bring me to a sense of wholeness and acceptance of both my spiritual and physical paths.

Language was inadequate—there should have been orchestras playing, suns rising, birds singing and waves crashing—it was just so far beyond anything I could possibly imagine. There were no words but every time I thought about this vision, I got chills. Nice chills.

As I woke the next morning and lay in that space between sleeping and waking, I heard these words spoken from the depths of my mind. *"I will fill you to overflowing, as a waterfall into a pool of ever-increasing size."*

Jesus knew how wake me with a smile and euphoric joy.

I was still working in the nursing home and was partnered occasionally to work with a particular staff member several times over the previous few months. During the time we worked together, a conversation occasionally began and would almost immediately hit a brick wall that we both bounced off. It seemed we were not able to have a conversation without our perceptions of reality clashing. Whenever I said something that challenged her, she answered with. "Just invite Jesus into your life."

I wasn't sure what she thought that would do.

About halfway through one shift, our conversation ground to the inevitable halt and in the silence that came from that I heard that clear, calm, strong voice speak in the depths of my mind. *"You cannot quench another man's thirst if he will not drink from your cup."*

Then I saw this vision.

My workmate stood in a sumptuously furnished room. At one side of the room there was a large panoramic window which was both the main feature and the only window to the room. The room itself was designed specifically for looking out this window and she was aware that the window looked onto the most beautiful landscape imaginable. People came to marvel at the beauty of this wondrous vista.

As one of the visitors, I got particularly close to the window. All of the previous visitors had stayed a respectful distance and expressed an appropriate amount of awe at the view.

She was uneasy at how close I was getting to her most prized window. I moved right up to it until my nose was almost touching it.

She was nervous and wanted to tell me to move back, and was about to do so when I turned and moved away. As I did so, I casually said. "Nice painting." As I left.

She was absolutely astonished by the insult and would have asked me to leave if I were not on my way out already. I felt her anger vibrating toward me, screaming, *How dare you say that!*

I saw myself leave but I was still there watching and experiencing her emotions and actions. She fumed that someone would be insensitive enough to say her worldview was a painting. She made a pact with herself never to let me back in to view her magnificent landscape.

She found herself annoyed that she couldn't get that ridiculous claim out of her mind. After fretting over it, she determined to put her mind to rest and prove me wrong.

She took a paint-scraper and moved close to the window, all the while wondering how anyone could be so stupid as to think what was visible through the window could possibly be a painting. The view through the window was vibrant and full of life; alive with light and colour.

She moved to one side of the window and brought the paint scraper into contact with glass. Tentatively, her heart in her mouth, she scraped the surface of the window.

She gasped in shock. It couldn't be. She scraped a little more and her stomach churned.

She put the paint scraper aside, took a deep breath, and brought her eye to the small hole she had scraped in the paint. Her knees felt weak and she jumped back from the window, almost falling, and stood there with her mouth open, her face in shock. How could this be?

She stepped back to look at the view through her beloved window. Words dripped from her mouth. "It can't be. That's impossible."

The once beautiful world she knew now seemed flat and lifeless.

She picked up the scraper and determinedly moved forward and didn't stop until the entire window was scraped clean.

She took a step back, then another. *How? What? I don't understand.*

A chill ran down her spine as understanding dawned upon her. What she had seen before, as a most wondrous vista, had been a painting of the landscape as seen from the back of the room.

The reality of the once hidden landscape now seen and experienced brought the painting into perspective. It had seemed so magnificent because she had only previously seen a representation of the truth. Now that the truth was before her, she could see the illusion for what it was.

I saw that vision with my work colleague and myself as the participants. Then, as soon as I understood that, I saw the whole thing repeated with me in the place of the owner, and Jesus as the one looking at the painting.

I understood that Jesus would expand my perceptions of reality beyond anything I could have imagined, and he would be the catalyst in expanding my level of self-awareness.

Chapter 33
Help!

I woke up one morning to see the same, or part of, a vision I saw a little while ago. I was underwater in the ocean, being tumbled over and over beneath the waves of a dark stormy sea, with no control, and no idea which way was up or down.

Okay! I understand. You're showing me that I have been in a state of tumultuous confusion, as I was shown in the vision of my lifeline during the car accident in 1996. But why are you showing it to me again? Maybe you're just showing me that you knew how I was feeling then?

I spent the entire day trying to work out why I would be shown part of a vision I had already seen, wondering what I was missing.

I went to bed and drifted off to sleep, again feeling like I was still being tumbled over and over in the stormy ocean.

I woke with the same vision circling in my mind—then it changed and I was struggling barefoot up a steep, wet, grassy slope. I was carrying all of my notes and diaries for this book tucked under my right arm, leaving only the left to help me to keep my balance and stop me from sliding backwards. I was not getting anywhere. The slope was too slippery for my bare feet. I couldn't get any traction and there was nothing for me to hold onto to pull myself up.

I was struggling with writing the book simply because the archangels and Jesus had encouraged me to. It was because they had asked me to do this that stressed me out and I felt like I was getting nowhere, just like in that vision.

These visions were frustrating, and not helpful.

What is the point of repeatedly pointing this out?

The following morning, I saw myself in my workshop at a table. I was working away diligently creating something. I couldn't see what I was working on which just increased my levels of frustration.

Three visions in three days and none of it made any sense.

All through the day of the third vision, they repeated again and again. Sleep came slowly that night with me still tumbling in confusion. I woke the next morning, and they were still there jumping up and down wanting my attention.

In that place of absolute frustration and helplessness, I prayed. "Help! I don't know what to do!"

As soon as I called, I heard his voice in my head. *"I am always here to help you, my son."*

It's hard to describe how that made me feel but I'll try. I had been lost in a state of total confusion, and all of a sudden the confusion was removed, and I felt that removal physically in my body.

Then I saw the three visions in succession, but with more understanding and detail. First I saw myself floundering underwater in the ocean. I was tumbled over and over under the waves of a dark stormy sea without control and no idea which way was up or down when I saw the light and headed for it. Then, I sat cross-legged on top of a calm sea bathing in the sunlight and drifting with the current. Seeing the light is the point where I came to understand what was going on in my life and so my confusion turned to calm.

Next, I saw myself climbing a steep, wet and slippery grass slope, but this time I wore spiked running shoes so I didn't slip and all of my notes were in a backpack so both my hands were free to climb. As I climbed, a strong hand reached down from above and Jesus said. *"Take my hand and I will draw you onto the path."*

I took his hand and he pulled me up to the path where he stood. That told me to follow his guidance and that of my visions.

Thirdly, I saw myself in my workshop, but this time I saw what I was making. I was sewing paper pages together, making them ready to bind into a physical book. I was working on this book to be precise, and my workshop had been changed around to suit.

Up until this point, I had been doing leatherwork instead of working on the book itself…stalling, I suppose. But in the vision, all of my leatherwork stuff that had been strewn around was neatly packed away to make space for me to write. It was time to get back to work on the book.

Even though I loved the idea of making my own books, this was all symbolic of an internal process.

The day following the three visions combined, I woke hearing these words spoken clearly in my mind. They came with a sense of calm. *"You were never meant to walk this path blindly, my son."*

As those words reverberated through my mind, I saw myself making books by hand that matched the one gifted to me by Archangel Uriel. I saw myself holding the first one in my hands—I smelled the leather. I felt the weight of the book and the texture of the red leather cover as I ran my fingers over it.

Having that book in my hands stunned me. It represented my journey and by simply being in my hands, it showed me that I was going to get to that place within myself where Jesus was guiding me. It gave me a sense of accomplishment beyond anything I could have imagined.

I thought to myself in amazement, *I did it.*

So I changed my workshop around to match what I saw in the vision and packed away all of my leatherwork gear, then started going through my notes and diaries again.

After a couple of days, I was lying in bed at nine o'clock at night and couldn't sleep. My mind was a mess. It felt like a flock of sheep trying to get through a doorway, all jostling for the best spot, pushing forward only to get stuck in a bottleneck. There were too many visions, dreams and prophecies trying to be noticed at the same time. In that state, I couldn't write anything, so I asked to have my guides help me understand how to do this.

Immediately, I felt a wash of calm and I saw what appeared at first to be a set of tarot cards set out in order, except they weren't standard tarot cards: they were my visions.

I understood at once that this was my story. All I had to do was go through my notes and diaries and set them out into chronological order.

"Thank you! Thank you! Thank you!"

I felt so relieved, and a bit silly for not thinking of that myself.

That night I had a dream that I was given instructions in code on how to find a buried treasure. I knew I was in a dream, and in the dream I spent a couple of months deciphering the coded message. The message had a strange set of specifications.

Those instructions told me that to find the buried treasure, I first had to construct a three-dimensional map and to make the map out of a cube of rose quartz about twelve inches square.

I was instructed to drill holes and make a series of saw cuts, each of a different depth, on all faces of the block. The cuts ran north-south and east-west.

The next instruction was to remove everything outside the bottom of the saw cuts and drill holes to expose the three dimensional model.

In my dream, that entire process took almost a full year to complete and the result was amusing and surprising.

After working on the piece of rose quartz, I stared at what I had sitting on the bench in front of me and laughed: I saw a life size replica of my head and my face.

Apparently I was my own buried treasure and I should love myself. That's what the rose quartz told me. Rose quartz also amplifies all the positive and negative vibrations around it, so this was also about amplifying love from the mind to the heart, or the heart to the mind. The rose quartz could also have told me to open my mind to my heart as the heart can amplify and clear the mind.

Jesus thought I was a buried treasure and he was sending me instructions on how to dig myself out. I kind of liked that. Of course all of the instructions associated with carving a replica of myself represented this book and my journey into self-awareness, as well as my mind/heart connection to the Holy Spirit where the dove took up residence within me.

While all of that was going on, I was also arguing. I kept hearing words echoing through the depths of my mind. They whispered to me the way a good clap of thunder could knock me off my feet.

For a long time, I tried to ignore those words but they simply wouldn't go away.

"Build me an ark."

"Build me an ark."

"Build me an ark."

And I would say. "No!"

That happened again, and again, and again.

"Build me an ark."

"No!"

"Build me an ark."

"I-am-not building-a-fucking-boat."

"Build me an ark."

"Aaarrrggghhh."

"Build me an ark."

"No!"

An Archangel's Gift

"Build me an ark."
"Not going to happen."
"Build me an ark."

It went on for months until I heard. *"Why not look up ark in the dictionary?"*

So I looked up *'ark,'* and the entry had a certain part of the description in bold: "**a vessel to contain the essence of Divinity**".

Not a boat then.

When I rechecked the entry a couple of days later, the bold part wasn't there, never had been, not physically anyway.

"Build me an ark."

Finally I wrote down what I had been hearing, hoping the voice would then leave me alone but as soon as I did, more came.

"Build me an ark of yourself."
"Build me an ark of yourself."
"Build me an ark of yourself."

The words thundered and whispered in my mind so I wrote them down, again thinking it was done, but again more words filled my mind.

"Build me an ark of yourself, and I will fill it."
"Build me an ark of yourself, and I will fill it."
"Build me an ark of yourself, and I will fill it."

Again I thought that was it but as soon as I wrote those words down, two more were added to the sequence with the same softness of an angel's touch and as subtle as a thunderclap.

"Build me an ark of yourself, and I will fill it to overflowing."
"Build me an ark of yourself, and I will fill it to overflowing."
"Build me an ark of yourself, and I will fill it to overflowing."

As I wrote that down, a feeling of love and smiles mixed with spring sunshine and the smell of fragrant flowers washed through me.

I guess I got it.

Just a couple of hours after sorting that out, I saw myself sitting alone in the dark of my workshop. A hand reached out and placed a ball of tangled fishing line into my hands.

Jesus' shadowy form stood next to me and he said. *"Here, untangle this."*

I struggled with the tangled mess for what seemed an interminable length of time, occasionally getting frustrated with trying to untangle it in the dark. I kept trying with varying degrees of patience and frustration and got nowhere.

At some point, a light began to shine from the darkness. A golden glow that I realised came from Jesus himself, who had been standing by my side the whole time.

With his light shining on me, I began to unravel the mess. I soon came to realise there was light enough and that there were two distinct threads in the tangle: one light and colourless, the other darker; the colour of shadow.

With the advantage of Jesus' light shining, I managed to get the mess untangled and the two threads separated.

What did this vision tell me? Sitting alone in the dark was my life without spiritual guidance.

The ball of tangled fishing line that Jesus handed me was what I had been writing. It also represented me untangling my heart and my light from the fears that I'd carried over the years. The tangled ball of fishing line was symbolic of the inner self that I had begun to unravel.

Unable to untangle the mess showed me that, at that point in time, I did not understand what was happening.

My ability to untangle the fishing line with the help of Jesus' light showed my acceptance of him into my life, and the difference that choice made, and that I was learning to surrender and trust in his guidance.

The two distinct threads showed the tumultuous confusion within me. That was caused by the battle between the dark and light sides of myself. That confusion, that battle, ended when I allowed Jesus to shine his light on me.

The two threads showed that I had been writing both the light and dark interpretations of the visions Jesus had shown me. That was my way of trying to distance myself from the task of writing this book.

It told me that with Jesus' help, I would be able to untangle and separate the two versions of the visions.

Once I understood that, I separated what I had written and printed out everything that had been written by the negative aspects of myself, and burnt them.

As I watched the pages burn, a couple of pages, fully alight, drifted up into the air and I remembered the vision I had all those years ago that told me I would do this. In that vision the negative aspects of self were bodies on a pyre.

An Archangel's Gift

Chapter 34
A Leap of Faith

The same vision kept running through my mind. It was like watching a full-length movie set in a time and place where there were no cars or planes, over and over again.

In the vision, I watched a wandering tradesman as he walked from village to village taking whatever work he could find. The tradesman walked down a country lane toward a mountainside. As he came close, he saw that built right up against the steep, cliff-like side of the mountain stood a large warehouse built of wood.

He entered the warehouse and found a store of timber both large and small inside it. The timber was cut, prepared and oiled. Two of the pieces of timber looked to be about sixty or seventy feet long. There were barrels of steel spikes and others full of wedges.

There were various sizes of hammers and pry-bars. Lengths of strong rope hung from pegs and pulleys sat on shelves.

An Archangel's Gift

At the back of the warehouse, where it joined the mountainside, there was the opening of a tunnel that looked a little like, but was not, the entrance to a mine.

Curious, although he knew the purpose of this place, he entered the tunnel whose floor was level with that of the warehouse, and was well lit from some source or other.

The tunnel ran straight through the mountain until it emerged, after several hundred yards, at a vertical cliff face a thousand feet above a fast flowing river.

Carved into the side of the tunnel were instructions that showed what the tools and materials in the warehouse were for. They were for building a platform that extended from the end of the tunnel, thirty feet out into open air.

The tradesman stood at the brink, looking out at distant snow-covered mountaintops. He turned, returned down the tunnel, and started to work.

Many weeks passed as he worked to drag the heavy timbers through the tunnel and build his platform as described by the carvings on the wall. At some point I stopped seeing the vision from outside and I became the tradesman. Finally, after all my hard work, the platform was finished and I stood alone at its end with the wind almost pushing me off my feet.

In the distance, I saw a dozen or more dragons of various colours frolicking in the thermal currents above distant mountains. As I watched, one of the dragons, a green the colour of emerald, broke away from its fellows and flew toward me. I saw a long sinuous neck, four legs tucked up for flying, and a huge expanse of wings. The dragon was magnificent and it was flying straight at me.

As it came closer, I prepared myself. The dragon flew just below the platform and stalled its flight, just as a voice spoke in my mind. *"Jump."*

It was the dragon's voice and I leapt into the clear morning air landing firmly on its back at the base of its neck.

Together we soared far above the landscape, with a perspective of the world below us that I could never have imagined even a short time ago.

I didn't like always being the focus of my visions; it made me feel self-conscious and I would have been much more comfortable if I could have directed their meanings elsewhere. Still, the meaning of this particular vision was clear.

The wandering tradesman was me and this vision showed me that after all the work I had done alone and would do alone on this journey, it would eventually come down to a leap of faith. After that, I would be able to see from a much higher perspective.

The wind almost pushing me off my feet shows the pressure I would feel writing this book.

That leap of faith, however, would be as scary as jumping off a platform onto the back of the flying dragon.

An Archangel's Gift

Chapter 35
What If This Is All Just Boot Camp?

I contemplated the visions and new levels of understanding I received as I unravelled their secrets as best I could. Another question rose in my mind. *"What is it in your nature to do?"*

Every time the question surfaced in my mind the answer was always the same. *"It is in your nature to remove obstacles from the path."*

And I would. If I was walking along a path and there was anything on it, I removed it.

It was also in my nature to puzzle out concepts and discover hidden worlds within worlds and interpret their meanings.

I really didn't know how that could be relevant but it seemed to want to be here. Perhaps writing this book was my way of removing the obstacles from the path that lay before me. That would fit in with the *Follow the earthen cascade* vision.

Jesus' words drifted through my mind. *"What if this is all just boot-camp?"*

If this was just boot camp then the future was going to be very interesting.

The woman I had warnings about a while ago was suddenly back. She called me at work, supposedly looking for someone else. I didn't think about it until later but she shouldn't have known I was at work, nor should she have known whom I was working with, but she did.

During the conversation, she asked me out for coffee and feeling sorry for her and thinking maybe the danger had passed, I agreed.

She continued to text me during the next few hours and coffee got stretched to coffee and a movie then to coffee, a movie, and dinner with kisses and hugs on the text messages.

By the next morning, I felt uneasy about the whole thing and thought I would go for a coffee and let her know that I could not see her anymore. Then, just as I had decided on this course of action, I saw myself walking along in the mall where I had agreed to go for coffee and as I turned in at the place we were supposed to meet, I was confronted by a huge, empty, windowless concrete room.

The empty space had the feeling of a warehouse wanting to be filled.

Symbolically, the empty room represented the woman I was supposed to go and meet. The absence of light told me that Jesus was not present in this situation or that I could fall into a great darkness, finding myself unable to get out. I knew that concrete would suck the heat out of my body and this was a warning for me, as heat represents the life force to me. In essence, it was a warning that, if I were to go against my guidance and get involved with this woman, who had lost her way spiritually speaking, she would suck the life force out of me. I wasn't prepared to be placed in such an emotionally vulnerable position, so I sent her a text message calling off the coffee, movie, dinner and whatever else she had planned.

Once that was done, I went and cancelled my phone number so she could no longer contact me.

If I was going to be having warnings in the form of visions, I was going to listen to them.

Soon after that, I was in the shower wondering why someone would chase me after telling them I did not think about them like that. I didn't get it at all.

While I was thinking about that, the *Follow the earthen cascade* vision began playing in my mind again but not as it was. Rather, it began where it ended with the three aspects of me moving confidently along the newly exposed path, which was open, clear, easy on the feet, and led into a lush and inviting forest that seemed to be only a few steps away. We moved along the path where time and distance seemed to play tricks on my mind. As we took those few steps toward the forest, our forms morphed together so that upon reaching the trees, we were one person housing three aspects in harmony.

As I watched this, Jesus words whispered in the depths of my mind. *"When the son becomes one, the child within will blend the three, all shall see the moon as one, and one will become all as one."*

I often felt like I was having these experiences so that I could write about having them. It also felt like I was filling out the *'relevant experience'* section of my resume. I was also learning to see myself through each vision and discover deeper meanings, which got very confusing at times.

Ever since Jesus came to me in visions and said to me. *"I know something about you that you are really going to like but you have to work it out yourself."* I'd felt like an aeroplane circling an airstrip in a holding pattern waiting for the fog to lift. And now, I thought I could see the fog thinning.

I finally knew what the straight line after the tumultuous confusion of my lifeline vision was. It was me doing exactly what I did while writing this book, except that instead of being afraid of the process and stalling for over ten years after the first set of visions and experiences, I embraced them as they occurred and allowed them to guide me.

I also felt during this process that I was in training in much the same way as I was in training as an apprentice bricklayer. In other words, *learning through experience.* Everything I saw and experienced lead me to my true self and a deeper relationship with Jesus.

An Archangel's Gift

Chapter 36
Muddy Water

Sometimes I saw visions with my eyes open, sometimes with my eyes closed. Neither was more prominent or distinctive and I saw things in lots of different ways.

On this day, with my eyes wide open, yet not seeing it with my eyes, I saw myself standing knee deep in the middle of an expanse of muddy water that stretched as far as I could see in all directions. The surface of the water was calm but I could see nothing of what lay beneath it.

I was looking at the vision from outside myself, as an observer circling myself and seeing it from all sides, while also being the participant and seeing it as though through my physical eyes. As I watched, the only sensations or emotions I had, were of calm observation. The vision was suggesting to me that I watch carefully what was happening.

Then, as I stood there knee deep in the centre, the muddy water began to clear. It cleared from where it touched me and then spread out in the manner of ripples from a stone dropped into a still pond, leaving everything once hidden beneath the surface, visible.

I looked at the vision wondering, *a vision of me standing in the middle of a pool of muddy water that slowly clears? What does it mean?*

I looked at the vision from my participant point of view, and then from the observer looking at it from all angles.

Then I got it.

At first, I had thought that the muddy water had cleared as I spent time in it, but then I realised that it had cleared, *because* it was me. This told me that no one else could work out the meaning of my visions for me. That I had to do it myself.

The vision also told me that to work out any vision, I had to step into the middle of it, be observant, spend a little time there; and clarity would come, leading me to an understanding of the visions.

Soon after that happened, I had a chance, again through my friend Jayson, to talk to Archangel Samhael and ask a question that had been bothering me for a while. "Some time ago, I asked Mickhael why I could go back in time to see the black horseman and Running Wolf, and I don't remember what the answer was but he said Jesus asked me to go back and watch the crucifixion."

"*Yes.*" Samhael waited patiently for me to continue.

"Whenever I have tried, I always see it through the eyes of a six year-old boy. Can you tell me anything about that?"

Samhael shifted the trance-channel's body slightly and said. *"There are levels to the answer, Edward. Is there any particular way that you wish for us to answer this? Would you like all levels covered or would you like that level which is most relevant to you now?"*

"I'll go for all levels."

Samhael's vessel gave a slight grin, even though the eyes stayed closed before he said. *"That could take some time. We'll choose the three most pertinent to your current level of understanding. There is an obvious explanation for what you experience when you attempt to go back and share that moment with the Divine essence known as Christ. That obvious answer is that an aspect, a spark, of who and what you are now, was back there at that particular time in the physical form of a child."*

"The second response of most relevance to you at this particular point in time relates to your own emotional state. Human beings are multi-faceted creatures that exist across numerous time frames. Depending upon that which has happened to a human being in its life, it will exist at a number of points in time."

"Though your year at this point is 2011, you do not exist solely and exclusively here and now at the age you are. You exist across multiple streams of time, multiple dimensions of reality,

and the mind is such that it can move with alacrity and great ability through these various dimensions. These points, along what is not exactly a river but an ocean. So, at some level, within you, the six-year old child who experienced certain important points in your life responds to what you were and who you were at the time of Christ's crucifixion. Do you understand so far?"

I said. "Yes." But I wasn't entirely sure I really did.

Samhael continued. *"The final most relevant point that we will address this night is around the concept of innocence. Your subconscious mind tells you that your concept of yourself, your experience of Edward Spellman in this lifetime, is corrupted. It is manipulated and affected by the views and the opinions and the information of others, as you perceive that information. Your highest self, through collaboration with your guidance and of my brother Uriel, remind you to view the world with a certain level of innocence. That which is taken from a human, from their childhood, is something that should never be forgotten in adulthood."*

"Reflect, Edward, and release some of the misconceptions and misperceptions that you possess now. Your adult mind is polluted. Let go of some of that. Approach the questions that you seek answers to with the mind and the heart, and the wisdom, of a child. Do you understand?"

"Yes, I think I do."

Samhael asked. *"Do you see how the information that you have been exposed to throughout your life has affected your perceptions?"*

"Yes."

Samhael gently delved. *"How deeply do you think this has occurred?"*

"Quite deeply."

"Do you feel capable of sweeping away the detritus of adulthood?"

"Yes, I do."

"Excellent. Good luck. Uriel reminds you to let go of your pain. It still shapes you to a certain degree and forms part of your misconceptions and misperceptions of who you are and what you are now. You are a work in progress but one we are happy to say has progressed quite some way, particularly since Mickhael's visit recently."

"Thank you."

Samhael steepled his host's fingers under his chin and asked. *"Are there other questions?"*

"I have another question." I said.

"Yes, Edward?"

"Is there anything you can tell me about the quote. 'When the son becomes one, the child within will blend the three. All shall see the moon as one, and one will become all as one'?"

"You already know the answer, my son. Would you wish us to elaborate further?"

"I would love you to."

"As part of the prophecy that was given some time ago that speaks of the union of faiths, however this prophecy has been

misunderstood. While it is ideal that such awareness is global, the awareness will not necessarily be global. Many religions exist. Many paths to God exist for a reason. The prophecy encourages those who seek to work actively with Spirit to embrace the concept of Oneness. That all faiths, all Gods, all Goddesses, depending upon which terminology you prefer, are in fact One. There is but one Divine Source. One Divine Architect: One Creator: without gender, without bias, without form, but most certainly with substance and meaning. That part of the prophecy encourages deep meditation and contemplation on that reality. Do you understand, or do you require further information?"

"No, I think I get it."

"Do you reflect on this reality?" Samhael asked.

"I do, yes."

"What are your ruminations revealing?"

"I believe people are starting to loosen up and accept the possibility of their being more than the organised religions tell them."

Samhael paused before he provided me with more guidance, then he said. *"You need to remove your contemplations from the macro and apply them to the micro. It does not matter what others think and it is not your job nor is it your responsibility, nor is it your divine destiny to persuade people otherwise. Your journey, my son, is to find the truth for yourself. Individuals who embrace this truth shine this truth, and then if they are to play any role in changing the perceptions of others, they do it through example. They do not do it through any other means."*

"The greatest benefit which you can have, the ultimate gift that you could receive from these contemplations is to own that reality, to explore it and to interpret it, to find the truth beneath the metaphor and to embrace that. You can only really achieve this through meditation, through quiet reflection and through a questioning mind that speaks and has conversations with others of a like spirit and you are surrounded by such people. Do you understand?"

"Yes, I do."

"We encourage you not to focus out. For many years, emissaries of Spirit have been encouraging you to focus in."

"I am starting to do that."

"Yes, it has been quite a process for you." Samhael conceded.

An Archangel's Gift

Chapter 37
Impatience

I was feeling a little impatient.

It was one of those days where I would like to be at that part of the *Follow the earthen cascade* vision where my anima opened this book to the page with a drawing showing my path into the future. It would be after I finished this book and had a printed copy in my hand, while at the same time I understood that I would not see nor understand what came next until this project was finished. I thought the feeling of impatience came from an inner knowing that the book was close to being done, or I hoped it was.

I was talking about my book to one of the doctors who visited the nursing home where I worked and she asked me one night. "Isn't it confusing with all those visions in your head?"

I looked at her a little stunned and a feeling of horror came over me as I contemplated a life without visions. For me, it would be like walking around without a head. "No." I answered. "I think life for me would be very confusing without them."

While getting people to bed in the dementia ward and thinking about the vision *Follow the earthen cascade,* I heard these words spoken clearly in my mind. *"All obstacles will be swept away. That which was hidden will be revealed."*

I imagined the obstacles I had put in front of myself being swept away as I moved through the process of becoming self-aware and reflecting upon my journey. The part of me that was hidden would be revealed through this process.

These words reminded me of a time, a couple of years before, when I worked at the nursing home with a forty-two year-old novice Japanese nun. Her English was not very good so she carried a small translation computer with her to help with the language barrier.

One morning during our break, she was translating or transliterating, the other staff members surnames into Japanese and giving them their meanings.

When she did my name, Spell-man, she gasped and said. "You magic man. You make magic for others by writing about yourself."

At that point, I had not told anyone at work I was working on a book. I was stunned and pleased by her interpretation.

Over the years, I recorded numerous messages but only put a few into this book along with my visions, just the ones that stood out as I went through my notes.

One of those that I did use came, again through Mickhael, when I asked him whether or not I had interpreted the symbols in a vision correctly, or if it was just my imagination.

"I will tell you something not many people know," he told me through a medium. *"That is how we communicate with you; through your imagination."*

"Does that mean that everything in my memory can be used by you to deliver a message through my imagination?"

"Yes, that's how it works. We deliver a message as energy to your soul, which, using your collective experience, translates it and delivers it through your imagination to your conscious self. Remember, Edward, that darkness communicates the same way as we of the Light: through your imagination, and a good man knows the difference as we will never ask you to do or say anything that would cause harm to others."

"Thank you."

Days passed. I slept, worked, worked on my book, slept again, then I was just allowing my mind to drift of its own accord as I woke and I saw myself stepping into an unfurnished white room with short dark grey carpet.

It was a space used solely for passing through. There was no furniture and no decoration on the walls. There were no windows or doors other than the one I entered through and at first glance, it appeared there were no other exits.

Yet, as I moved into the room I saw an opening that was at first hidden by an angle of wall. The room was elongated and L-shaped with the inside corner cut off forming another wall. It felt like it was inviting me to pass through it rather than anything else. The opening in the room was on my left hand side and was just an opening from floor to ceiling with no door or obstruction of any kind; it opened onto a busy modern airport. Then there was a mountain meadow through the door, and then another landscape, and then another and another.

It was getting easier to understand my visions; maybe all my practice was paying off.

This vision told me that where I was in my life was just a place to pass through and when I had, I could choose any destination and nothing would stop me.

I enjoyed waking up to a vision like that; it was a good way to start the day. With the vision sorted, it was time for a shower and then some breakfast.

Would it sound weird if I said I talked to my visions and that my visions responded? Probably, although it would be more accurate to say we communicated with each other.

When I posed a question, I either saw a fresh and relevant vision, or previous ones would get together and behave like a tarot reading to give me an answer. If I didn't understand, they would just keep at me until I got it.

If they appeared just once, it meant I understood what they said.

Sometimes what I understood the first time was right for me at that particular time and then, after a few more years of contemplation and life experience, the vision would return so I could take it to a deeper level. The deeper level required me to undergo life experiences, assimilate them into who I am and contemplate the new interconnections.

I suppose it's a bit like maths in that there is always a deeper level waiting to be understood.

An Archangel's Gift

Chapter 38

The Framework for the Rest of My Life

I kept seeing myself, both when I was sleeping and while I was awake, building a house.

No! Not a house, the framework *of a house.*

In those dreams and visions, I was building the framework of a circular house out of raw green logs. The basic structure was set out on concentric circles like ripples on a pond. And I felt excited. Excited in a way that I hadn't felt for a long time. It felt like something was about to happen that I had been waiting on for a long time.

I saw myself preparing each log by stripping it of bark, smoothing out any rough spots, carving the joints and fitting them into place.

I watched as I made the joints and fitted the logs. All of the logs came together without nails, bolts or screws, as all of the joints were self-locking. Each log that was added made the logs that were already in place, more secure and stable. Once complete, it would be able to withstand any storm.

An Archangel's Gift

The vision told me that the framework was the framework for the rest of my life. It meant that all of the experiences I have had, some of which are in this book, coupled with the experience of writing this book, made up a framework of the skills and attributes I gathered along the way.

As soon as I had written that down, I had another vision. This time I saw myself as a medium sized chestnut horse with big white patches, prancing along a beach in shadow. While at the same time, I was the horse prancing down the beach. I revelled in the feel of the sand beneath my hooves, the wind in my mane, the swish of my tail, and the smell of salt in the air as I drew it into my nostrils.

I moved along the beach until I came to a weathered outcrop of rock: there was an archway in the rock that had a barrier of sorts across it. It looked a little like the surface of a soap bubble with the sun shining on it, even though it was at the centre of the arch where the sun didn't reach. As I touched the barrier with my muzzle, I felt a slight resistance, not much, just a little and I walked forward, pushing my way through.

I saw this from both sides of the outcrop at the same time as well as from the point of view of being the horse. From one point of view, a chestnut and white horse walked into the barrier while from the other point of view, a sparkling white unicorn, with a longer main and tail than the horse had, and feathery hair around his fetlocks, walked out of it onto another beach.

The colours were brighter on this side and the whole world sparkled with a life force I had never seen before. As the unicorn, I could see further and with greater clarity and purpose. The air was sweet, clear and refreshing. I breathed in deeply and felt a profound sense of magick and wonder fill me.

From this vision, it looked like I was in for a big change in my perceptions of self and reality. It was not that the horse changed into a unicorn, it was just that once I walked beneath the arch, my true nature was exposed.

The barrier, a particular point in space and time, kept the shadows of the past from moving into my future present, and the shadows of the past were fear and doubt. It seemed I would finally be able to leave them behind, or see them transformed as the unicorn symbolised as it came out of the barrier.

The colour of the unicorn, pure white and sparkling, told me that my connection with spirit would be deeper and more profound than I could have imagined.

I spent a lot of time meditating and contemplating the visions I had seen and every so often when I meditated to gain an understanding of one vision, another turned up. In this case I had just been lying on my bed contemplating the time when this task was completed, and thinking about the possibilities this journey would create in my future when I saw myself standing on the top of a mountain looking out over the countryside I had travelled through to get there. The way I had come was rough and tangled but when I looked down over the landscape, I could see that there was never any other way to get to where I was.

As I looked about, I saw that this mountaintop was at the edge of a high plateau and to continue forward, I did not have to go back down the mountain.

The vision told me that having come this far, the journey would not be as difficult in the future. It also showed me the obstacles I had overcome to get that far.

Chapter 39
The Stone Passageway

I saw myself walking through an underground, stone lined, perfectly straight passageway about eight feet high and six wide. It had regular cut stone walls, a rusty-orange floor paved with two-foot square stones and stone ceiling. There were no shadowy corners, no nooks or crannies and no side passages. It was three blocks wide and set out like the squares on a chessboard with the light even throughout the length of the passageway.

Although the ceiling was made of slabs of stone that spanned the passageway from side to side, and were as wide as three paving stones, there was no feeling of weight, or pressure, from above. Ahead I saw an open doorway, while behind me, the passage was lost in a mist.

As I came to the end of the passage, there was an open doorway leading to a large room built in the same manner as the passageway. The room was about fifty to sixty-feet long, about thirty wide, and twice the height of the passageway. There were no windows and yet the light was of the same quality as the passage.

I looked about the room while standing in the open doorway and noted the three other doorways. All four doors were of the same configuration, although the other three were closed. They were large stone slabs that operated by sliding vertically.

I had a strong feeling that if I stepped into that room, I would not be able to go back the way I came. Still, I knew that the only way to find out what came next was to step through.

With some trepidation, I stepped into the room and the door immediately slid shut behind me.

There was no feeling of danger, rather a feeling of being safe and protected pervaded me, and yet I knew I had a lot of work to do before getting out.

As I moved about the room, I found there were specific tasks to undertake and puzzles to solve. They were the keys to opening the end doors. I set to work and successfully completed each obstacle.

As I finished the last puzzle, two end doors were triggered. Water rushed in and flooded the room and I was forced toward the ceiling. Soon I was gasping for air, about to drown. I took my final breath as the water engulfed me.

The fourth door opened, triggered by the weight of the water. I whooshed through with the water and landed on my feet. I was in an environment without walls. There were no boundaries at all, except for a floor and I knew intuitively that the only reason there was a floor at all, was to ensure that I didn't freak out.

I could only describe that place as limitless and still, that word seemed extremely inadequate. But, how could I describe a limitless reality?

Upon reflection, this vision presented like an adventure movie with me as the main character. The stone passageway I was walking was my life; the mist was my past; the light was my spiritual guidance. The passage being straight with no side tunnels or passages told me I was guided to a specific place represented by the doorway and the room beyond it. The straight passage also showed me that no matter what my choices were, this doorway was always where I would end up.

The walls of the stone passageway represented the limitations of my perceptions of both self and reality. The lack of pressure from above showed the quality of my guidance and that although I was being guided in a specific direction, I was not being pushed or coerced. I had undertaken the journey of my own free will.

The doorway itself represented the point in my life where I had the choice to undertake the journey into self-awareness or stay hidden within the mundane.

An Archangel's Gift

Stepping through the door represented a commitment to walking into the unknown; having faith and embracing the consequences and lessons awaiting me.

The door sliding shut showed me that once that choice had been made there was no turning back. Moving into the room showed that my perceptions of reality expanded well beyond what they had been, once I had committed to this path.

Once in the room, I was confronted with a series of tasks and puzzles which perfectly reflect how my own brain and spirit needs to move through obstacles and unlock the clues to continue to move on my adventure of self-discovery.

Then the room was flooded with water and I felt like I was drowning. The water was emotion and the journey itself had often left me feeling like I was in too deep and drowning.

Then the fourth door was triggered and I was washed out into a limitless place. It was the whole process of discovery and reflection that generated so much emotion—that feeling like I was drowning and overwhelmed—and that was the catalyst for the next step.

Once beyond the room, I stood on another stone paved area that I knew was only there to comfort me—to give me a footing of sorts, especially since I didn't understand the limitlessness that this place represented.

The fourth door also represented my final barriers and resistance to whatever comes after, which is shown as a path beyond the fence in the vision, *Follow the earthen cascade*.

Once through this door, everything changed.

An Archangel's Gift

Chapter 40
The Farmer and His Sheep

This story flowed into my mind in much the same way as a drinking glass is filled by a water jug. It took time to settle and become clear. Once it did, this is what I saw.

There was a modern day farmer with a flock of sheep that he kept on a large block of land, perhaps a thousand acres, with a single boundary fence.

At the beginning of this story, all of the sheep were newly shorn, then, as the story continued their fleeces grew until it was again time for shearing.

The farmer did not stay with his sheep all the time; allowing them to graze at will then rounding them up regularly to check and count them and do the things that sheep farmers do.

In about the centre of the farm there were holding yards where he brought the sheep regularly to check them. Whenever he did this, there was inevitably one sheep missing. It wasn't just that there was one sheep missing; it was always the same sheep. He didn't look to be any different than any of the other sheep. And when he was with the other sheep he behaved in much the same way they did.

The farmer and his sheep dog went to search for the sheep and always found him and brought him back, reluctantly, from outside the fence. Then he would look until he found the hole where a wombat or kangaroo had pushed its way through the wire squares of the stock fence leaving a hole big enough for the sheep to get out and he repaired it, only to have the same thing happen again.

After this pattern repeated several times and the sheep all had full fleeces, it came time for shearing and again there was one sheep missing; but this time no matter how much the farmer looked, he could not find the sheep nor could he find the hole in the fence where he had escaped.

So, I asked in my mind. *What does the farm where the sheep graze represent?*

The answer came clearly. *"The farm is a representation of the three-dimensional reality you are taught to exist in."*

And the fence?

"The fence is the fundamental concepts and beliefs that you have been programmed with throughout your life that contains and supports the limitations of a three-dimensional reality."

What about the farmer; what does he represent?

"The farmer is ego. Ego built the fence. Ego maintains and repairs the fence. And it is ego that brings you back from beyond the fence on those occasions that you have slipped through."

Okay! So, what is beyond the fence?

"That which is beyond the fence consists of the spiritual, metaphysical, and mystical that constitutes the experiences you have written about in this book. That which is beyond the fence is outside of the parameters that define and contain three-dimensional reality."

And the sheep?

"The sheep is you, Edward."

What about the sheep's wool?

"The wool has several meanings. At the beginning of the story the sheep is shorn, and ends with a full fleece. This shows the correlation between your self-esteem and this book. When you began, your self-esteem was almost non-existent. When you finish this project, which is as always, a reflection of your journey into self-awareness, your self-esteem will have been regrown so to speak. It also represents the personal energy that others have taken from you in the past."

That means that the holes in the fence are my forays into the spiritual, metaphysical and mystical dimension beyond the fence that are the experiences I have written about here?

"Yes, that is correct."

An Archangel's Gift

If I understand this correctly, that would mean that, once my journey into self-awareness and this book are complete, I will have shaken off the programming that inhibits me and contains me in this three-dimensional reality enabling me to move freely amongst the spiritual, metaphysical and mystical dimension, that preside beyond the fence?

"Correct again, my son."

Thank you.

This does not mean that I exist only in this three dimensional reality. It simply means that the paradigm that has defined me would no longer contain me, and the new paradigm with which I define myself, includes the physical and metaphysical, as well as the spiritual and the mystical.

The realm within the fence was not separate from that beyond the fence, it simply did not acknowledge what was beyond the fence while existing within it.

Chapter 41
God's Workshop

Sometimes when visions came, they threw me into shock; at other times, I accepted them calmly without question.

When visions took hold, they came visually, audibly, or both. They could come with touch, taste, smell, sound, and with other senses that I had no name for. This particular vision slipped into my consciousness with a sense of calm and somehow, a sense of timelessness.

I saw myself walking toward a large windowless building with a massive three-piece yellow door. Each section of the tri-fold door was about thirty feet high and twelve feet wide.

In my right hand, I held a golden key shaped like a stylised shooting star, looking much like a comet with a tail burning through the atmosphere. It was solid gold and heavy. It measured about three inches long, two wide and a little wider than it was deep. It was an electronic key with a button in the eye of the comet, and fitted neatly into the palm of my hand with familiarity.

As I approached the building, which was a workshop, a group of angry people walked past.

To my surprise they were angry with me and one of them broke away from the group and approached, saying. "It's not fair that you have the key. Why don't we get to have the key? It's just not fair."

I had no answer for him. I didn't know why I had the key myself.

He then re-joined his group, grumbling about the unfairness of it all. Soon they were out of sight and my attention returned to the workshop.

I stood before the three bright yellow tri-fold doors of the workshop. They were the size of a two-storey house and completely water tight. I raised the key, pointed it at the doors and pressed the single button. The doors softly folded into themselves, opening to my right and revealing the workshop for me to explore.

There was no sign above the doorway, but if there had been, it would have read, *God's Workshop*.

As I moved into the workshop, my mind flipped and twisted a little until it finally settled down. Stepping through the door was like stepping to *some-where* and *some-when* else; or perhaps, *every-where*, and *every-when* else.

Just inside the doorway and on my left, was a machine that looked a little like a large industrial lathe but was much more than that. As I examined it I knew that it, along with the entire workshop, existed in all dimensions of time and space. It had always been there and it would always be there.

On my right, there was another machine, if you could call it that, which looked completely organic. It looked as though it had been grown. It exuded power and a soft light that seemed to contain stars the size of dust particles. Every time I looked at it there was something different about it that my mind could not quite grasp. Still, I knew what it did: it rearranged matter. This machine changed the structure and density of basic molecules, changing one element into another.

In this workshop, anything could be made, and by having the key, I had permission to create anything I wanted.

It seemed to me that the main purpose of this vision, apart from showing me that some people would be jealous and want the key, was to pose the question. *If you could make anything you want, and you can, what would it be?*

That's easy. I wanted to finish my journey into self-awareness and make my own copies of my book.

This vision also reminded me of a local preacher who came to my door several times to talk about Jesus and God. I often liked to talk to preachers but usually didn't answer their questions with much detail.

On the last occasion that this preacher came, he had his wife with him and we began to discuss Jesus and the Bible, but on that day, I felt like answering their questions as honestly and completely as I could rather than holding back as I usually did.

And I soon learned my mistake.

As the preacher asked me about Jesus, I answered him honestly. The more I revealed to him about my relationship with Jesus and my experiences, the redder his face became. Anger was coming off him in waves and it appeared that he was quite upset that he had not had these experiences with Jesus, whom he loved and followed.

The preacher's wife saw that our conversation was upsetting her husband, so she took him by the hand and dragged him away.

That was the last time the preacher came to my door and it was a good lesson, and warning, for me.

I believe anyone can have the key to God's Workshop if they are willing to enter into themselves, do the work of self-exploration and take leaps of faith.

Chapter 42
Buried in a Landslide

I was down by the waterfront having a coffee and staring out across Moreton Bay. I was watching the sunlight glinting on the water when I saw a vision of Jesus and me.

Jesus tore frantically with his bare hands at the loose stone of the landslide that had buried me. The harder he tried, the more loose stone fell to replace what he had moved.

Deep inside the rock fall, I was safe and cocooned in a protective bubble, as though there was a force field around me.

The rocks that made up the landslide were all the same type, a dull shiny grey colour. They were small, with none more than half the size of a person's head; their edges and surface were as soft as soapstone.

Safe in my cocoon, I was oblivious of Jesus efforts to dig me out. As I watched him attack the loose rock, I could feel his emotions. I recognised his feelings from the time I lost my youngest son when he was three and a half years old, at the Brisbane Expo in 1988. My son had slipped his hand out of mine and it took about a thousand years, or ten minutes, to find him. The feelings I experienced were the same Jesus was allowing me to feel from him in the vision. Just feeling those emotions directed at me was enough to make a grown man cry; which I did.

After what seemed like a very long time, Jesus stopped trying to dig me out and he drove a long, narrow steel rod into the landslide and through to where I was in my cocoon. The steel rod was a guide for me to follow and find my way out.

The rock around me in my cocoon did not behave in the same way as the rock on the outside where Jesus was. Where he was, the rock was loose and fell at the slightest touch. Inside where I was, the rocks had the magnetic properties of magnetite, so I could move them from one side of my space to the other, and could move along the guide Jesus had provided for me. Every now and then, I moved a rock, then stopped and looked around, then moved some more without any real idea where I was going, or even that I was buried under a pile of rock. I was just following the guide to see what happened.

This vision left me in a public café with tears running down my face and my throat all choked up so I got up and left utterly embarrassed. The emotions of the experience were overwhelming.

Edward Spellman

Jesus had been trying to get me out since 1997, for the past fifteen years, though probably more. It was some landslide.

An Archangel's Gift

Chapter 43

A Farmer, His Son, and the Knight in Golden Armour

This story was projected into my mind like a movie onto a screen. It was set in the Middle Ages, in the time of knights and chivalry.

In the first scene, a farmer and his young son walked along a dirt road that was wide enough for four people to walk abreast, headed for the annual fair. They were excited; the farmer because he was taking his son for the first time, and the son because he had never been.

As the two came upon the oak forest they would pass through on their way to the fair, there was a knight, covered head to toe including a visor over his face, in golden plate armour. He stood squarely in the middle of the road and blocked their way forward.

As they drew closer, the knight, who stood alone in the centre of the road without weapons or horse, said to the farmer. "If you want to pass, you must fight me or give up your son."

The farmer replied politely. "I will not fight you nor will I give up my only son."

As I watched the vision unfold the knights' voice sounded strangely familiar but I just couldn't place it.

With that, the farmer and his son turned around, disappointed, and returned to their farm.

The following year, they took the same path to the fair, only to again find the golden knight blocking the road. And again, the knight said to the farmer. "If you want to pass, you must fight me or give up your son."

Again the farmer politely replied. "I will not fight you nor will I give up my only son."

As they did the year before, the farmer and his son returned to their farm to wait for another opportunity.

For a third time, the farmer and his son tried that same path, and again for a third time the golden knight blocked the road. And again they returned to their farm without reaching the fair.

Each year, the farmer and his son would set out for the fair and each year they would find their road blocked by the golden knight.

At first, they tried other paths but no matter which path they tried, the golden knight blocked the road.

As the well-known paths did not work in getting them to the fair, they began to try other ways. They tried walking across the fields and the golden knight was there. They tried sneaking through the forest and the golden knight was there. They tried slipping through the countryside at night and again the knight blocked their road.

Sometimes they wondered if all the golden knight did was think of ways to block their path.

The son grew into manhood, and this year he and his father walked together along the same path on which they had first met the golden knight; and there he was again.

As happened every time they met him, the knight spoke these words. "If you want to pass, you must fight me or give up your son."

Before the farmer could reply, the son stepped forward and said. "I challenge you to a duel."

And the vision was gone.

As I looked at this vision, my lifeline kept flashing on and off in front of my eyes telling me that it was connected. The three characters were all aspects of me. The farmer was me before the accident in 1996, ageless and me at forty-two. His son, on the other hand, did age and represented me over the past twenty years. The knight in golden armour was my future self; wearing the armour the Goddess gave me in Chapter 19, My Suit of Golden Armour.

The confrontation with the knight was a confrontation with my future self. The forty-two-year-old aspect held me back until I was ready to confront myself, and my future self blocked my path until such time as I was ready.

The confrontation itself was when I put everything else aside and studied everything I had written and completed my book, like the hermit monk in the mountain cave of Chapter 31, Your Past Points to Your Path.

Chapter 44
Redcliffe Lagoon

In August 2005, I had an experience early one morning, which I diligently recorded in my diary, then conveniently tucked away under the rock at the back of my mind to forget. Just last week, I was going through my diaries and found it. As I read what I wrote, it all came flooding back.

I remembered writing that I felt as though there was something missing in my mind; that I could find the place where it should be but could not find whatever it was. It felt to me as though I had spiritual amnesia. Finally, what had been lost to me had been found.

Sometimes, the things I saw and experienced were so far beyond my perceptions of reality that I needed to be protected from them until I could handle them without either running screaming for the mountains or feel my ego collapse. This was one of those experiences.

When an experience like this came along and I was not ready for it, it came with a sort of spiritual sedative to soften my reactions and give me time to assimilate it into my psyche. Sometimes it felt like a shock absorber, and sometimes it came with a time delay lock, as this one did. So, here is what took place in Redcliffe Lagoon.

I woke early that morning to a phone call cancelling my shift for the day. Seeing as how I was already awake; I jumped in my car and took the ten-minute drive to Suttons Beach.

When I got there, the tide was low and the water cloudy, full of seaweed with thousands of blue jellyfish both in the water and on the beach. Unfamiliar with the ocean, I opted not to swim with all the jellyfish and the seaweed. Luckily, just past the northern end of the beach, there was a landscaped, manmade lagoon, so I headed there for my emersion in salt water.

I swam around for a little while, enjoying the feel of the cold water on my skin and moving through it. Standing neck deep in the crystal-clear water of the lagoon, I heard the lightest feathery touch of a voice in the back of my mind encouraging me to let go and float; to surrender and have faith.

I don't float. Never could get that. Before that day, I had never been able to just lie back, relax and float. Oh sure, I could do my version which necessitated constant movement of both hands and feet. Sometimes I could manage with just the hands but if I stopped moving, because of the stress and tension in my body, I would slip beneath the surface and get water in my mouth and up my nose.

Standing neck deep in the water, however, and listening to the feathery touch of the voice within me, I was receptive.

"Shut your eyes." I heard in my mind.

So I shut them.

"Have faith. Surrender." The voice instructed.

Then I felt the feathery touch again, although not as a voice this time but exerting a force directly against me. It touched me on the forehead, right between the eyes and pushed. It pushed me with a force that was so gentle it was like the lightest touch of a feather, like it should not be able to move a single inch and yet, strong enough to move mountains.

It delivered with its push, the knowledge that it would allow no harm to come to me and then for the first time in my life, as I was pushed backwards, I lay back in the water in faith and surrendered—and I floated!

I floated there for a little while. It was wonderful. Then I stood and opened my eyes, saying in my mind, *Okay, I get it. I need to have faith and surrender.*

The voice came back. *"Close your eyes."*

And again, came that push on my forehead, and again I floated, in the womb of creation. *"Stay a little longer—have faith—surrender."* Whispered in the depths of my mind.

An Archangel's Gift

When I came to the realisation that this was the way to live my life, I was allowed to stand and open my eyes.

Pleased with my realisation, I decided to leave the lagoon. There were fresh water showers there to wash off the salt water and that was where I was headed. I could see the shower, a couple of picnic tables, a public toilet block, a bridge over an artificial creek, a gardener's shed and a pedestrian ramp that zigzagged through the trees up to the street about thirty feet above.

The voice whispered to me again in the water. *"Close your eyes."*

So I closed my eyes.

As I moved in the water with my eyes closed, the water grew deeper. Standing on my tip toes, it reached just between my top lip and my nose. *"Have faith—surrender—faith—surrender—faith—surrender—now open your eyes."*

The number of steps I took should have seen me well out of the lagoon but I was still in the water up to my top lip. I opened my eyes and looked out over the lagoon and the ocean beyond. I was facing in the opposite direction to the shower, looking out over a calm stretch of ocean, with blue sky above, and with a feeling of hope and promise in my heart, and warmth in my belly.

I turned around and again headed for the shower.

"Close your eyes."

So again, I closed my eyes and walked toward the shower. As I walked, I noticed that the water did not get shallower as it should of as I approached the steps. *"Open your eyes."*

And once again I was facing the ocean with the steps and shower directly behind me.

When I went home, I understood that I was being told that if I have faith and surrender, Jesus would guide me in a direction completely different to the direction I thought I was going. And that open ocean—that direction Jesus had in mind—was many times more expansive than the world I lived in.

So, what did I learn? That I should have faith, surrender, allow Jesus to guide me, and I would end up somewhere completely unexpected.

Could be fun.

An Archangel's Gift

Chapter 45
Follow the Ripples

A few years ago, Jesus said to me. *"Live a life that makes you proud of the life you have lived."* But a fear of mine kept returning so I wrote it down. It was the same fear I had since starting this project—losing myself—losing my identity—being controlled by something else—of being like a puppet who is aware of what was happening but with no choice and no control.

As soon as I wrote that, I heard his voice again. *"I understand your fear, my son, and in a way, you are correct. You have both lost, and yet still have within you, the you who began this journey. It was your ego that feared its own loss—this still lingers a little and has reared its head at this time because you are so close."*

"Let me assure your ego that it will have experiences and see sights that it would never have or see if it did not sit in the passenger seat—I do not seek to control you, my son—only to guide you along the path you and I discussed before you were born, and then again on the day of your car accident."

An Archangel's Gift

I felt a warm, smiling energy flow through my body. When Jesus smiles at me, it feels like spring sunshine with the sweet, floral, honey like fragrance of the Madonna lily in full bloom.

Jesus said, *"Do you feel that? I know you do and also, I know you understand that it is me that touches you."*

On the following Tuesday morning, I was editing my writing at the computer. When I thought it was time for a break, I put on some incense, put on an Enya album, grabbed my headphones and lay down for a bit. Almost as soon as I relaxed, I was on a path on a cliff face the colour of charcoal. The path was a flat, level ledge, where the cliff stepped back about four feet and stretched off behind me until it disappeared into the distance. As I looked back where I had come from, I saw that it was spotlessly clean with no obstacles at all. The path before me, however, was covered with rubble but I was almost at the end. The path disappeared around a corner to the right, from where a golden light glowed, adding another dimension to the normal light of the day.

As I listened to Trains and Winter Rains by Enya, I watched myself pick up rocks that blocked the path and threw them over the edge. Then I found a straw broom and swept the path clean. I felt nervous, and more than a little excited. It meant I was nearly done.

The path along the cliff was almost clear, meaning that I had cleared away almost all of the blockages in my path.

Not long after this vison, I found myself asking, for the thousandth time, *Why?*

He answered in the depths of my mind. *"Why does the tree grow? Because I planted the seed."*

While I was thinking about Jesus' answer to my question of why, I saw him a little distance away standing beside a pool of still water. He was dressed as he was when he came to me years ago in the forest clearing, a knee length robe and wrap around sandals.

There was a smooth black stone the size of a golf ball in his right hand—he drew his hand back, looked at me and smiled as he threw the stone high into the air above the pool.

The stone sailed slowly in an arc that ended as it landed in the centre of the pool sending ripples out in all directions across the surface.

"Why are there ripples on the pond?" he asked with a glint in his eyes. *"Because I threw the stone. Why did I throw the stone? To cause the ripples on the pond. Follow the ripples, my son."*

I can do that, I thought to myself.

Ok! I asked myself, *"So, what did I do or where did I end up after not being killed?"*

What came to mind first was actually being killed in the car accident and meeting Jesus and Archangel Uriel and the one I call Farronell. By following the ripples, I was saved by my guides so I could die and meet them—so I could be shown why I am here and come back and continue along my path.

The next question had to be. *What did I come back and do?*

I came back not only to write this book but have the experiences that were necessary to create it. To take the journey into self-awareness.

By following the ripples, I can see that I was saved so many times to allow me to finish what I came here for, to learn, to grow, and to deepen my experiences in life.

And for some unknown reason, to put my experiences into this book.

Chapter 46
Why Not Me?

For years, I wanted a translation of the prophecy that Jesus gave me and I then carved into my staff, but who could do it?

Silly me. I had the staff and the only copy of the prophecy, so maybe I was supposed to interpret it? (The full prophecy without the interpretation is in Chapter 17, Bleeding Fingers.)

So I did my best.

1:1   In the days that number nine,

I had always found this first line confusing, then I realised that if I followed Jesus advice to, 'follow the ripples', it was always meant to be confusing. Having seen that means I no longer need to be confused, so it must be time for me to interpret the prophecy. Remembering that from confusion comes clarity.

1:2   from the New World will arise, the prophet Elijah,

The New World is the world that arises from the new world-governing paradigm of generosity and benevolence. Elijah is the Biblical Old Testament prophet. I have no idea what form this will take.

1:3   to bring forth and unfurl the Faith of the One,

The prophecy encourages those who seek to work actively with Spirit to embrace the concept of Oneness. That all faiths, all Gods, all Goddesses, depending on which terminology we prefer, are, in fact, One. There is but one Divine Source. One Divine Architect. One Creator, without gender, without bias, without form, but most certainly with substance and meaning.

1:4   to express the Word of Divinity,

To write, speak, or otherwise express the Word of Divinity.

1:5   at a time when darkness and light
1:6   fight for dominance in the world of man.

Seems pretty straight forward to me. Darkness is represented by avarice and light by generosity and benevolence.

Edward Spellman

2:1 The angels will walk once more
2:2 upon the world's surface,
2:3 and their children shall sing celebratory songs,
2:4 announcing the return of newness,

With the help of the angelic realm, this world is going to change.

2:5 and the rebirth of Jerusalem.

This speaks of the New World that comes out of the new, world-governing paradigm of generosity and benevolence.

3:1 The Goddess' reign shall be complete,
3:2 with the Lords once more,

These two lines mean no more patriarchy—nor matriarchy—there will be balance with the male and female aspects of Divinity in harmony. This connects to or reflects the words tattooed in runes on my forearms. "Not alone through the female aspect of divinity, nor alone through the male. Only through the harmonious union of the two shall humanity prevail."

3:3 and rebirth, and beginnings beyond beginning,
3:4 will affect the world and the people of all lands.

The world will be made anew under the influence of the new paradigm. All countries. All cultures. All peoples.

An Archangel's Gift

4:1 Light will be seen for eternity throughout all lands

We are moving from an age of darkness into an age of Light.

4:2 as darkness creeps amid despair

Darkness is getting desperate because it foresees its own end, and it is darkness that is in despair.

4:3 attempting to dissemble,

Spreading lies and disinformation.

4:4 and wake the fears of many,
4:5 the fears of many are really the fears of one,
4:6 and the one, is self.

Darkness tries to wake the fear in everyone. Everyone is responsible for their own fears and darkness will do everything it can to keep us afraid as that is how it holds power over us. When we conquer our fears, the power of darkness is no more. What darkness fears most, is humanity no longer being afraid.

5:1 Dreams of heaven many must sell,

In these times you will see many selling a connection to the Divine.

5:2 the crimes of one, will bring about
5:3 the announcement of hell.

Again, I don't think any translation is necessary for these two lines.

6:1 False prophets ride upon the winds of fear,

This speaks of false prophets using fear to sell salvation. They are easy to spot as, if they are using fear and or are selling salvation, they are false. You can't buy salvation. It is not for sale and yet it is available to everyone, for free, and without exception.

6:2 Dragon's Breath lights fear,
6:3 in the hearts of man and woman.

Dragon's Breath, also known as Ley Lines, are the lines of a planetary energy grid enveloping the Earth. As people become more sensitive to these energy lines, those that don't understand what they are feeling will fear them.

7:1 Avarice is the core to understanding the old,

Avarice was and is the governing paradigm of the age that has just come to, or is about to come to, an end.

7:2 the old is the core to establishing the new.

The old paradigm points to the new, as the battle between darkness and light is between opposites, so the paradigm for the new, is the opposite to that of the old. The establishment of the new comes from a paradigm of generosity and benevolence.

7:3   as stars fall and worlds quake,

> *As those who have held themselves above others through the exercise of avarice fall and have their perceptions of reality shaken to the core. Their worlds will topple in much the same way as an earthquake topples buildings.*

7:4   the brilliance of truth may come too late.

> *The truth that may come too late is that avarice is not a beneficial path and that humanity needs to change its ways.*

8:1   Fear of prophecy and truth lie still,
8:2   the heart of man,
8:3   a stone to be shattered at will.

> *Much of mankind is still afraid of prophecy and truth. Those false beliefs that we hold close to our hearts will be shattered easily.*

9:1   In a land where the tall poppies grow,
9:2   and are ruthlessly cut asunder,

> *In Australia we have what is called 'tall poppy syndrome' where people who become prominent in the public eye are often attacked for nothing more than that they are successful.*

9:3   rise the stars of the Southern Cross,
9:4   to bring forth an end to plunder.

> *This means a group of either five people, or organisations, banding together to work for the benefit of all. They will help bring an end to the plundering of the planet we live on.*

10:1 Of peace on Earth, and goodwill to all,

This line is a signature of sorts. It is Jesus saying, this is my prophecy. Which is fair enough because he is the one who gave it to me. It is also a direction humanity can choose to take.

10:2 some may know it,
10:3 but it will bring about the downfall of all.

Some people will understand what is going on in the world, but everything is going to change. Everything. It will shatter our perceptions of reality.

11:1 All That Is may come again,

All That Is, is the Divine Source. The Creator. The Divine Architect, and they are all One, and that is the concept that is coming. That we are All One. (The faith of the One.)

11:2 that which was holds no power.

That which was, is avarice. That power which has gripped the world for so long is drifting into the past. Losing its grip. Losing its power, to the new paradigm of generosity and benevolence.

11:3 Travel the roads that lead to the heart,
11:4 from the heart, the soul doth start,
11:5 from dreams and wishes, life becomes art.

Here are another three lines that require no translation so follow your heart. Follow your dreams and wishes.

An Archangel's Gift

12:1   Peace is the gift that cannot be held,

Peace is the gift that cannot be held because it is a gift from the Divine and it cannot be held from us. All we need to do is claim it.

12:2   the sound of the bell, announces the fall, of hell.

The sound of the bell is a shared epiphany. The fall of hell is the fall of the old patriarchal society dominated by avarice. And the arrival of Peace on Earth through the new world governing paradigm of generosity and benevolence.

Epilogue

Now that I've come to this point in my journey, I wonder at the purpose behind Uriel giving me the book and Jesus and the archangels encouraging me for all those years to write it.

Now that I'm here and I take another look at my *lifeline,* it shows me that from this point on, my life will be continually more and more different to anything I have previously experienced. It took me years to learn to trust the guidance in my visions, dreams and whispers in the depths of my heart; to trust that Jesus was always with me, and always would be.

Writing this book has already changed me: it has changed the way I think and the way I look at the world. I now have a library of symbolic language to guide me forward that will undoubtedly grow along the way.

Messages from Spirit always have multiple layers. A message can be relevant and mean one thing today then, after some time and more experience, the message deepens and opens other layers.

I suspect I will be unravelling the messages I have already gotten, to say nothing of the ones to come, for the remainder of my life.

I also understand that if I ever need help, all I need to do is ask. I have learnt that the angels will not intervene unless invited; and once invited, they are here even though at times I may not recognise their assistance.

One of the most important things I have learnt along the way was said by Archangel Mickhael, *"One of the biggest lies ever told was that good things come to those who wait. It would be more accurate to say, 'Good things come to those who put in the effort'. Once you ask for our help and begin, we will match your effort."*

A little while ago I asked Jesus why he kept encouraging me to write my book.

He replied, *"What's the point of having a story if you don't share it?"*

Then he said, *"Where your story goes, faith grows."*

It is my hope that, as writing this book has taught me to have faith in my spiritual guidance, so too will it help others to have faith in their own.

Edward Spellman

About the Author

I began this journey the day I died. It started with the perspective that the physical body is animated by the soul and I found that my soul had been knocked out of my body.

I tried very hard to push my experiences down and forget them. However, that was not to be and Spirit had other plans for me.

It's important to add that I relate to the Divine by using the term Spirit. While I believe in God, and some might call me a Christian (and some might not), the term God is a limited term to me. The term Spirit has fewer religious connotations and, in my mind, is less restrictive.

Once the concept for this book was presented to me, I avoided it for ten years. I wrote about anything else, anything but what was to go into this book. The idea terrified me. I was terrified of exposing my deeper self, both to myself, and to the world in general.

After ten years, however, slowly, step by step, I embraced this project: my personal journey into self-awareness with this book as a tool to achieve it.

Writing this book took eighteen years and throughout the experience I realised that this is not just something I am going to do and then move on.

An Archangel's Gift

The process of understanding my experiences and how they have affected my life is one of the reasons I am here; and the process of creating this book will always be something that will significantly influence and empower my life.

I expect life is about to become rather more interesting than it has been. I see a door about to open...*I wonder what I will find as I step through?*

Edward Spellman, 2016

The photo opposite is a replication of a vision I saw while making a copy of this book. It means that there are multiple layers of meaning to the things I have written about. And as I got to this point in the book and had come to an understanding of it, the next layer began to present itself.

It also means that the deeper I go, the more magickal it will become.

Edward Spellman

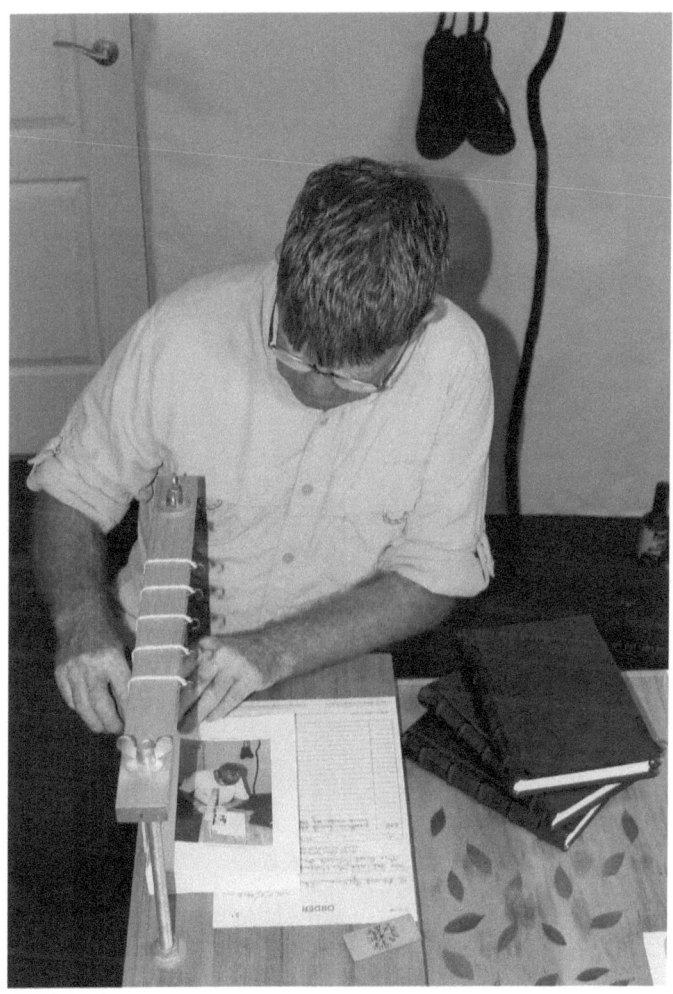

My Workshop by Edward Spellman, 2016.

An Archangel's Gift

Thank you for reading my story.

www.ingramcontent.com/pod-product-compliance
Lightning Source LLC
Chambersburg PA
CBHW032302300426
44110CB00033B/275